AMERICA the BEAUTIFUL

IOWA

By Deborah Kent

Consultants

Loren N. Horton, Coordinator, Field Services, State Historical Society of Iowa

Robert L. Hillerich, Ph.D., Bowling Green State University, Bowling Green, Ohio

CHILDRENS PRESS®
CHICAGO

Historic buildings, many with ornate architectural details, line Pella's business district.

Project Editor: Joan Downing
Associate Editor: Shari Joffe
Design Director: Margrit Fiddle
Typesetting: Graphic Connections, Inc.
Engraving: Liberty Photoengraving

Library of Congress Cataloging-in-Publication Data

Kent, Deborah.
   America the beautiful. Iowa / by Deborah Kent.
      p.   cm.
   Includes index.
   Summary: Introduces the geography, history,
government, economy, industry, culture, historic
sites, and famous people of Iowa.
   ISBN 0-516-00461-1
   1. Iowa—Juvenile literature. [1. Iowa]
I. Title. II. Title: Iowa.
F621.3.K36   1991   90-21276
977.7—dc20   CIP
                                              AC

Ducks and winter squash at a farm in Calamus

TABLE OF CONTENTS

Chapter 1

IN THE HEART OF THE HEARTLAND

IN THE HEART OF THE HEARTLAND

On the wall of the Equitable Life Insurance Building, an immense mural greets visitors to downtown Des Moines. The painting is a vast map of the state of Iowa, spreading 30 feet (9 meters) from the Missouri River to the Mississippi. Its artists have created not merely a map, but a stunning panorama of Iowa life. The mural is a collage of scenes: great cargo ships on the rivers, small towns with sturdy frame houses and tree-lined streets, and endless, rippling fields of corn.

Iowa lies within a fertile belt of land that cuts across the middle of North America. This immensely productive agricultural region is often called America's heartland. In the American consciousness, the heartland stands not only for high crop yields, but for the basic values upon which the nation was founded.

Iowa devotes 93 percent of its land to farming, and most of its other industries are closely tied to agriculture. It is a state of small cities and rural county seats, where the church supper is a major social event, children are expected to help with chores after school, and neighbors pull each other through hard times. Iowans are deeply committed to education, to family and community, and to the democratic process.

Urban Americans often idealize Iowa as a sort of time capsule, embodying all the virtues of a saner era that ended in the rest of the world long ago. Certainly, Iowa is not immune to modern problems. But it is a place where families generally stick together and community spirit remains strong. Stretching between the Missouri and the Mississippi, Iowa lies at the very heart of America's heartland.

Chapter 2
THE LAND

THE LAND

"I loved my towns, my cornfields, and the home of my people. I fought for it. It is now yours. Keep it as we did. It will produce you good crops."

Speaking at Fort Madison in 1838, Chief Black Hawk of the Sauk Indians commended Iowa's fertile land to the white settlers. In honor of Black Hawk, Iowa is nicknamed the Hawkeye State.

GEOGRAPHY

Iowa lies in the heart of the American Midwest. It is bordered by Illinois and Wisconsin to the east, Minnesota to the north, South Dakota and Nebraska to the west, and Missouri to the south. The Hawkeye State is shaped somewhat like a battered box, with irregular boundaries on the east and west. Iowa spreads over 56,290 square miles (145,791 square kilometers), ranking it twenty-fifth in size among the fifty states.

Many people who have never lived in Iowa believe that the state is tabletop flat. But this notion is woefully incorrect. In fact, most of Iowa's landscape is made up of gently rolling hills. In the northeast rises a craggy, almost mountainous area so rugged that Iowans call it "the Switzerland of America."

Many thousands of years ago, a series of glaciers crossed and recrossed the land we now call Iowa. The glaciers were great mountains of ice, sometimes more than a mile (1.6 kilometers) thick. The grinding action of these giant glaciers leveled

The Driftless Area, nearly untouched by the glacial activity that smoothed out most of Iowa's land, is marked with rugged hills and cliffs.

mountains, filled in valleys, and deposited the fertile topsoil that today supports the state's thriving farms.

Glacier activity left Iowa with three distinct land regions: the Young Drift Plains, the Driftless Area, and the Dissected Till Plains. The Young Drift Plains cover the north-central part of the state. When the first white pioneers arrived, the Young Drift Plains were mostly swampland. Enterprising farmers drained the swamps and found some of the world's richest soil. The Driftless Area is the rugged, semimountainous section in the northeast. Glacier activity was slight in the Driftless Area. Today, the region is a landscape of stark, tree-covered hills and cliffs that overlook the Mississippi River. The Dissected Till Plains cover the remainder of the state. Glaciers deposited great loads of soil, or till, on this region, and left it with endless rolling hills.

Some of the nation's richest soil is found in Iowa.

Poet Robert Frost once said that Iowa's rich black soil "looks good enough to eat without putting it through vegetables." A staggering 93 percent of Iowa's land is used for farming. Among the fifty states, only Nebraska has a greater percentage of its soil devoted to agriculture. The Young Drift Plains region, where corn is the primary crop, contains the richest soil in the country. But farms thrive nearly everywhere in the state. Even the Driftless Area, which is too rugged for row crops, supports productive dairy farms.

RIVERS AND LAKES

Iowa's eastern and western borders are formed by the two mightiest rivers in the United States. The eastern border is defined by the broad Mississippi, which Native American people once

The Mississippi River forms Iowa's eastern border.

called the "Father of All the Waters." The state's western border is drawn by the Missouri, itself a branch of the Mississippi. All of Iowa's many rivers and streams empty eventually into either the Mississippi or the Missouri. A low ridge that slants across the western half of the state serves as the divide between the two rivers. Rain and melting snow west of the Mississippi-Missouri Divide flow toward the Missouri; precipitation that falls east of the divide drains into the Mississippi.

The Des Moines River, a branch of the Mississippi, is central Iowa's most important river. Nearly 500 miles (805 kilometers) long, the Des Moines drains nearly one-fourth of the state. Other major tributaries of the Mississippi include the Turkey, the Wapsipinicon, the Skunk, the Iowa, and the Iowa's tributary, the Cedar. The branches of the Missouri, in the western part of the state, tend to be shorter and more swift-flowing. Primary Missouri

Iowa's many rivers include the Maple (left) and the Volga (right).

tributaries include the Floyd, Little Sioux, Boyer, Maple, Nodaway, and West and East Nishnabotna rivers.

Iowa has no large natural lakes. Most of its lakes are concentrated in the northwest near the Minnesota border. Beautiful Spirit Lake enriches Dickinson County. Other natural lakes that are popular vacation spots are Storm Lake, Clear Lake, and West and East Okoboji lakes. Scattered throughout the state are artificial lakes created by dams in river systems. Large man-made lakes include Coralville Lake, on the Iowa River; Lake Red Rock and Saylorville Lake, on the Des Moines River; and, largest of all, Rathbun Lake, on the Chariton River.

PLANTS AND ANIMALS

Pioneers entering Iowa found marshlands in the north and tall-grass prairies in the south and west. In pioneer times, trees grew

Kalsow Prairie (left) and Hayden Prairie (right) are protected natural prairie areas.

only along the riverbanks. On the prairies, late summer grasses rose above the pioneers' wagon wheels, and sometimes even went past their horses' heads. A host of animals, from the lumbering buffalo to the wild turkey, lived in the grasslands. With human settlement, the prairie grasses disappeared, as did most of the animals they harbored. Today, the prairie grasses that once blanketed the state grow only in protected preserves. At Hayden Prairie, in Howard County, visitors may picnic on a patch of natural prairie and imagine a time when seas of grass such as this stretched from horizon to horizon.

Less than 4 percent of Iowa is forested. Most of the state's few thick woodlands are in the Driftless Area. Yet throughout Iowa, trees grow along riverbanks. Common hardwoods include oak, maple, and hickory. Cottonwoods grow mainly in the sandy soil of river valleys. Wildflowers such as bloodroot, marsh marigold, and many species of violets light up the state in springtime.

Luna moths (left) and butterfly weed (right) are among the animals and plants found in Iowa.

The white-tailed deer is the largest animal surviving in Iowa's natural areas. Smaller animals, such as skunks, rabbits, opossums, and raccoons, can also be found. Mink hunt along marshy streams. Quail, grouse, and pheasant nest in fields and pastures. Iowa serves as a resting ground for Canada geese and other migratory waterfowl. Fishermen pursue smallmouth bass, trout, bluegill, catfish, and walleye.

CLIMATE

Typical of the American Midwest, Iowa has many sweltering days during the summer and long periods of frigid weather in the winter months. The highest and lowest temperatures ever recorded in the state illustrate this variance. In January 1912, at Washta, the thermometer dropped to minus 47 degrees Fahrenheit (minus 44 degrees Celsius). On one day in July 1934, in Keokuk,

Most of Iowa lies under snow from December to late March.

the temperature rose to a scorching 118 degrees Fahrenheit
(48 degrees Celsius). Iowa weather is also subject to sudden,
dramatic changes. A drop or rise of 50 degrees Fahrenheit
(28 degrees Celsius) over a twenty-four-hour period is not
uncommon, especially during the spring.

   With no mountains to serve as a barrier, high winds often howl
over the state's farm belt. Iowa is sometimes struck by violent
tornadoes. Soil erosion due to wind activity is a constant problem.
Some experts believe that Iowa loses more topsoil each year
through wind erosion than does any other state.

   Iowa usually enjoys ample rainfall to nourish its many farms.
Average annual rainfall is 36 inches (91 centimeters) in the
northern part of the state and 26 inches (66 centimeters) in the
south. Most of the state lies under snow from December to late
March. Snowdrifts in the north often pile high enough to bury a
parked car.

Chapter 3
THE PEOPLE

THE PEOPLE

*[Iowa] combines the qualities of half a dozen states,
and perhaps that is the reason why it seems, more to its own
people than to others, the most undistinguished place in
the world. . . . Iowa has never had the rampant boosterism of
Kansas and Missouri. It has always been far too deprecating
and self-doubting for that. Among all the meek states Iowa,
which has been on the fence geographically, politically,
religiously, and aesthetically, has been the meekest.*
—Iowa novelist Ruth Suckow

POPULATION

The 1980 census reported 2,913,808 people living in Iowa. In
terms of population, Iowa ranks twenty-seventh among the fifty
states. Though the number of Iowa citizens increased by 3 percent
from 1970 to 1980, the decade of the 1980s presented a different
picture. The estimated 1990 population figures indicate that Iowa
is one of only seven states that lost population between 1980 and
1990.

Iowa ranks fourth in the nation in percentage of people over the
age of sixty-five. The state's population declined during the 1980s
because the number of deaths caught up with the number of
births. Many senior citizens left Iowa for a warmer climate. In a
phenomenon known as the "brain drain," thousands of well-
educated men and women in their twenties sought new jobs out
of state.

Although Iowa is one of the nation's most productive farm
states, the majority (59 percent) of the people live in cities and

towns. Until 1960, however, more than half of all Iowans lived in rural areas. The largest concentration of people in the Hawkeye State live within the "Golden Triangle." On a map, this triangle can be drawn from Des Moines, in the center of the state, to the Mississippi River cities of Dubuque in the north and Keokuk in the south. Five of the state's six largest cities lie in the Golden Triangle region.

Iowa has about thirty cities with populations greater than ten thousand. In terms of population, the six largest cities are Des Moines, Cedar Rapids, Davenport, Sioux City, Waterloo, and Dubuque.

WHO ARE THE IOWANS?

The majority of Iowans are white, and most have ancestors who came to America many generations ago. About 98 percent of Iowans were born in the United States, and 80 percent were born in the Hawkeye State itself. About one Iowan in five can trace roots back to Germany.

African Americans make up 1 percent of the state's population, as do people of Hispanic origin. A small but growing number of Asians live in the state. A small number of Native Americans, most of them belonging to the Mesquakie tribe, live near the Iowa River in Tama County.

Most Iowans belong to one of the Protestant denominations. Roman Catholics, however, make up the largest single religious group in the state. Major Protestant groups include Methodists, Lutherans, Presbyterians, and Baptists. Lutherans predominate in the rural areas of northern Iowa. Catholics are concentrated in the Mississippi River cities. The state's major cities have small Jewish populations. Amish and Mennonite people live in the farming areas. The Amish renounce modern conveniences such as automobiles and televisions, and their horse-drawn buggies can sometimes be seen on rural roads.

POLITICS

The towns and cities of Iowa shine with prosperity. Slums are few and crime is rare. Iowans take great pride in their families; the state's divorce rate is among the nation's lowest. The Iowa school system is a model of success. Iowa has the highest literacy rate in the country, with 99 percent of its adults able to read and write.

Educated, committed citizens keep Iowa's quality of life high. Hawkeye residents are so concerned with their government that many churches hold political discussions before services.

The Republican party has been the driving force in Iowa politics since the Civil War. But Iowa Republicanism swerves from the norm. While Republicans from other states often favor a strong national defense and a tough foreign policy, Iowa Republicans, reflecting the will of their people, tend to be "doves" (a political term for one who favors negotiation over war). Voters in the state were decidedly against America's involvement in the Vietnam War. The state's most influential newspaper, the *Des Moines Register*, regularly advocates policies leading to the reduction of world armaments.

Political writers often attribute Iowa's "dove-ish" attitudes to good business sense. Iowa farmers sell an enormous amount of wheat and corn to the Soviet Union and to eastern European countries. To the farmers, maintaining friendly relations with good customers seems to be a sound idea.

Once every four years, presidential hopefuls and hordes of

Elk Horn's annual Tivoli Fest honors the area's Danish heritage.

reporters swarm into the Hawkeye State as Iowa voters prepare to hold "the caucus." The Iowa caucus, or primary, is the nation's first step in electing the president. During the caucus, voters gather in schools, public buildings, and even private homes to express their choice for a national leader.

The Iowa caucus carries little weight in the actual nominating process, but it is the first test of a candidate's popularity. In 1975, Governor Jimmy Carter of Georgia spent several nights in Iowa farmhouses while he campaigned. Iowa voters liked the man from Georgia, and his victory in the caucus was the first step in Carter's long road to the White House. During the 1988 caucus, Iowa's white voters gave a surprising 9 percent of their votes to black candidate Jesse Jackson, giving new credibility to his bid for the White House.

Chapter 4

THE BEGINNING

THE BEGINNING

From a plane, there is no mistaking the great Woman Mound for what it is—an enormous female figure reclining with arms outspread. The Woman Mound, on the Turkey River near the town of Clayton, is one of some ten thousand earthen structures scattered across the state of Iowa. These mounds are the most visible reminders of the many peoples who lived in Iowa before the arrival of the first Europeans.

THE FIRST IOWANS

Wandering bands of hunters and gatherers moved into the land we now call Iowa some twelve thousand years ago. They were the descendants of Asians who had long before crossed the Bering Strait into North America. Using spears tipped with carefully chipped and flaked stone points, they hunted bison, elk, and other game. As time passed, these nomadic people learned to plant such crops as corn and squash. Gradually, they gave up following the herds and settled in more or less permanent villages surrounded by cultivated fields.

About two thousand years ago, people known to archaeologists as Mound Builders began erecting burial mounds in Iowa. Usually the mound was built over a shallow grave in which the dead person was laid to rest with an assortment of weapons, tools, pottery bowls, and ornaments. Many of the mounds that survive in Iowa today are cone-shaped; others take the forms of birds or animals. The mounds vary greatly in size. Some are only 3 feet (0.9 meter) high and a few feet in diameter. The Woman Mound, on the other hand, is 135 feet (41 meters) long.

Archaeologists are not sure why the mound-building cultures disappeared. But by the time the first Europeans reached Iowa, in the late 1600s, the culture that had produced these mounds had disappeared. Native Americans living in Iowa in the 1600s could only shake their heads unknowingly when asked who had built the strange hills of earth.

At one time or another, some twenty Native American groups lived in present-day Iowa. Most of these groups belonged to either the Siouan or the Algonquian family of tribes. Tribes within each of these families had similar but distinctive languages and customs.

The Sauk (or Sac) and the Mesquakie (or Fox) were Algonquian tribes. They were driven westward during the seventeenth and eighteenth centuries by white colonists and by people of the fierce Iroquois Nation. Weakened by constant warfare, the Mesquakie eventually formed a union with the Sauk. Most of the Sauk and Mesquakie settled along the Rock River in present-day Illinois, but some crossed the Mississippi River. A large village arose near the present-day town of Montrose, Iowa.

Siouan tribes migrated into Iowa and Minnesota from farther south. Among the Siouan tribes of Iowa were the Missouri, the Oto, the Dakota (or Sioux), the Winnebago, and the Iowa (or Ioway). The Iowa, for whom the state is named, called themselves the Pahucha. They were referred to as the Iowa by their enemies, the Sioux. The name has been variously interpreted to mean "one who puts to sleep" or "beautiful land."

Most of the Indians in Iowa lived along streams and rivers, leaving vast stretches of tall-grass prairie nearly uninhabited.

Nineteenth-century photographs of Sauk Indians

They traveled the waterways in birchbark canoes or heavier wooden dugouts. The men hunted and fished, and the women tended the fields. Wars erupted frequently between neighboring tribes, and a man was expected to prove his bravery through daring deeds in battle.

THE COMING OF THE EUROPEANS

In May 1673, a French trader named Louis Jolliet and a priest named Father Jacques Marquette set out from the shore of Lake Michigan in two birchbark canoes. With their five crewmen, Marquette and Jolliet hoped to explore the great river that lay to the west. After a month of rugged traveling, they finally reached

Marquette and Jolliet, exploring the Mississippi River in 1673 (above), became the first Europeans to set foot on Iowa soil.

the Mississippi, and glided southward between its high, wooded bluffs. When they spotted a footpath on the river's western bank, they left their canoes and went ashore, becoming the first known Europeans to set foot on Iowa soil.

Marquette and Jolliet followed the path to a cluster of Indian villages. These people, who belonged to the tiny Peoria tribe, spoke an Algonquian language that Father Marquette understood. When the explorers assured the Peoria chief that they were enemies of the Iroquois, he exclaimed, "Never has our tobacco tasted so good, never has the river been so calm, never has the sky been so serene, nor the earth so beautiful as on the day when you Frenchmen have come to visit us." He did not guess that in the end, white men would prove a more devastating enemy to the Iowa tribes than the Iroquois had ever been.

In 1680, French explorer René-Robert Cavelier, Sieur de La Salle, sent an expedition under Michel Accault and Father Louis

Hennepin to trace the course of the upper Mississippi River. Two years later, La Salle claimed for France the entire Mississippi River system and the land it drained. He named this sprawling territory Louisiana, after French King Louis XIV.

For nearly a century, French traders visited the Indians of Iowa, exchanging kettles, guns, and whiskey for valuable beaver, otter, and mink pelts. But the French made no attempt to farm the land or to fortify it against invaders. In 1762, France ceded to Spain the portion of the Louisiana region west of the Mississippi River. Yet while faraway rulers dickered over the land, life proceeded almost undisturbed for the Indians of Iowa.

Sometime late in the 1700s, a Mesquakie Indian woman discovered deposits of lead along Catfish Creek. Mesquakie women began mining the lead, which was used to make gunshot. In 1788, word of the mines reached Julien Dubuque, an enterprising French fur trader. Dubuque asked the Mesquakie chief to let him take over the mining operation, explaining that he would smelt the lead into bars, or "pigs," and ship them to market at the settlement of St. Louis. When the chief refused, Dubuque threatened to set Catfish Creek on fire. According to legend, Dubuque had some of his companions pour oil on the water farther upstream. As the oil slick drifted past, he tossed a burning stick into the creek. The water roared into flames, and the terrified chief promised to give Dubuque anything he wanted.

To please the Spanish monarch and further secure his position, Dubuque called his holdings the "Mines of Spain." Indians continued to mine the lead, and shared in the profits when it was sold in St. Louis. When Dubuque died, the Mesquakie buried him with all the ceremony accorded a great chief.

In 1800, France regained control of the part of Louisiana that it had given to Spain in 1762. Three years later, Napoleon Bonaparte of France sold the entire Louisiana region—which spread from the Mississippi River to the Rocky Mountains—to the new American nation for $15 million. Iowa now belonged to the United States.

STAKING THE CLAIM

President Thomas Jefferson was eager to learn more about the vast land his nation had acquired. In 1804, Congress authorized Meriwether Lewis and William Clark to lead an expedition from St. Louis up the Missouri River. After battling the fierce current for two months, the explorers met a group of friendly Missouri and Oto Indians on the Nebraska side of the river. They held a meeting opposite a prominence on the Iowa side that was known from then on as the Council Bluff. Farther upstream, one of the expedition members, Sergeant Charles Floyd, died, apparently of a ruptured appendix. He was buried at the site of present-day Sioux City. Floyd was the only member of the expedition to die on the long journey, and the first United States soldier to be buried west of the Mississippi River.

As Lewis and Clark explored the Missouri River, another expedition set out from St. Louis. Lieutenant Zebulon Pike followed the Mississippi north, looking for sites where forts might be built. He soon discovered that French and British traders had warned the Indians of his approach. When his expedition reached the mouth of the Des Moines River, he wrote in his journal, "It is surprising what a dread the Indians in this quarter have of the Americans. I have often seen them go around islands to avoid me and my boats. It appears to me that the traders have taken great pains to impress upon the minds of the savages the idea of our being a very vindictive, ferocious and warlike people."

Pike recommended two possible sites for forts on the Iowa side

While exploring the Mississippi, Zebulon Pike (above) recommended the hill known today as Pike's Peak (left) as a site for an American fort.

of the Mississippi. The first was the bluff where the town of Burlington stands today. The second was a hill in present-day Clayton County that is known today as Pike's Peak. Since Pike discovered this peak before the famous mountain in Colorado that bears his name, Iowa can claim that it has the *original* Pike's Peak.

Ironically, the army paid no attention to Pike's suggestions when it was ready to build a fort in Iowa. In 1808, Lieutenant Alpha Kingsley set off up the Mississippi River with orders to erect a fort and a trading post at the mouth of the Des Moines River. When he reached this spot, however, he decided that the low-lying land might flood in the spring. Instead he chose a location several miles farther north. In a letter to the secretary of war, Kingsley wrote that the site had a spring that would furnish plenty of drinking water and offered a fine view of the river. He failed to notice that a ridge farther inland offered an excellent view of the fort.

Left: Sauk Chief Keokuk
Above: Reconstructed Fort Madison

In 1812, the United States went to war with Great Britain, and was forced to defend its claims on the upper Mississippi. During the War of 1812, Kingsley's Fort Madison (named for President James Madison) proved a major liability. Spurred on by the British, the Sauk and Winnebago Indians held the fort under siege through the summer of 1813. "[The Indians on the ridge] can actually arrange for the execution of any plan they choose without being discovered," wrote the fort's commander, Thomas Hamilton. "They can come down upon us like a flash of lightning." At last, hungry and demoralized, the American troops crept away from the fort in the dead of night. Crawling on hands and knees, they sneaked to the riverbank, slipped aboard waiting boats, and fled downstream to St. Louis. The last men to abandon the stockade set it on fire, and the ill-fated Fort Madison vanished in a tower of flames.

The United States defeated the British in 1814, and the upper Mississippi remained securely in American hands. Yet, when an Italian adventurer named Beltrami traveled along the river in 1823, he found only one sign that white people had ever lived in Iowa—the grave of Julien Dubuque.

THE BLACK HAWK PURCHASE

The people of the new American nation had an insatiable hunger for land. By the early 1800s, complaining that the Atlantic Coast was overcrowded, Americans began pushing into the unsettled territory farther west. Year by year, more forests fell and farmers' plows broke fresh furrows in a steady march toward the Mississippi.

In 1830, President Andrew Jackson authorized a treaty with the Sauk and the Mesquakie. The treaty forced the Indians from their home on the Rock River, giving them in exchange a fertile, 50-mile- (80-kilometer-) wide strip of land west of the Mississippi. One young chief, Keokuk, pointed out that the land west of the river was good and urged his people to remain at peace with the whites. Reluctantly, the Indians crossed into their new territory along the eastern edge of present-day Iowa.

But Chief Black Hawk, the sixty-five-year-old veteran of many bloody wars, counseled the Sauk to resist white encroachment. In the spring of 1831, he led a band of followers back across the Mississippi to their old village of Saukenuk. On the eastern side of the river, the women planted their crops. Within a few months, however, Black Hawk was forced to sign another treaty, and he and his people returned to Iowa once more.

Even after this retreat, Black Hawk would not give up hope. When a young brave reported that the British in Canada were

In 1832, Sauk and Mesquakie Indians, resisting the American government's attempts to move them from Illinois to the Iowa region, fought in what became known as the Black Hawk War.

anxious to aid the Indians in a war against the Americans, Black Hawk began to make new plans. In April 1832, he and his followers recrossed the Mississippi for the second time, and set off toward Canada, certain that they would meet friendly British reinforcements on the way. But neither the British nor other Indian allies came to their aid. Black Hawk's party met the United States Army on the Bad Axe River in present-day Wisconsin. So many Indians died in the battle that one observer claimed that the river ran red with blood. Black Hawk was captured and sent to St. Louis in chains.

To punish the Sauk and the Mesquakie for breaking the treaty, the United States government deprived them of the rich grasslands along Iowa's eastern margin and sent them still further west. Within less than twenty years, virtually all Indians had been driven out of Iowa. The land along the Mississippi, which had earlier been granted to the Sauk and Mesquakie in perpetuity, was opened to American homesteaders. Farmers and government officials dubbed this tract of land the Black Hawk Purchase.

THE TWENTY-NINTH STATE

"[The land] is one of great beauty," wrote army Lieutenant Albert M. Lea in a promotional pamphlet in 1836. "It may be represented as one grand rolling prairie. . . . For convenience of navigation, water, and timber, and richness of soil, for beauty of appearance, and for pleasantness of climate, it surpasses any portion of the United States with which I am acquainted." Lea was the first writer ever to use the term "Iowa" in print to refer to the land between the Mississippi and the Missouri.

At the time of the Black Hawk War, probably not more than fifty white settlers occupied Iowa. But word of the rich new territory quickly traveled eastward, and a stream of eager farmers set out for the Black Hawk Purchase. Loading their cows, pigs, and chickens onto flatboats, they ferried across the Mississippi.

The first towns in the Iowa region sprouted along the Mississippi River. Dubuque arose in 1833 at the site where Julien Dubuque once mined for lead. Burlington was founded by a pioneer merchant, who named it after his hometown in Vermont. Another river town was named after George Davenport, a trader who had lived in the area since 1816.

When the Black Hawk Purchase opened for settlement, Iowa's legal status was uncertain. In the spring of 1834, Patrick O'Connor, an Irish miner from Dubuque, shot and killed his cabin mate. In a makeshift courtroom, he admitted that he had done the deed, but argued, "Ye have no laws in this country and ye cannot try me." Nevertheless, O'Connor was found guilty and sentenced

Iowa's earliest towns, including Dubuque, grew up along the Mississippi River.

to death. His friends appealed to President Andrew Jackson, who replied that he had no authority to pardon a man in the ungoverned territory. O'Connor hung for his crime.

The O'Connor incident highlighted the territory's need for an official governing body. In June 1834, Congress annexed Iowa to Michigan Territory, placing it within reach of federal law. Two years later, when Michigan became a state, the land of present-day Iowa became part of Wisconsin Territory. Finally, in 1838, Congress carved out a vast expanse of prairie land, stretching from the Missouri line to the Canada border, and designated it Iowa Territory.

President Martin Van Buren appointed a serious-minded man named Robert Lucas to serve as governor of the new territory.

When Lucas arrived in Iowa, he was greeted by a chorus of shrill cries from Burlington, Davenport, and Dubuque, as each of the tiny settlements clamored to be chosen as territorial capital. The governor selected Burlington as the temporary seat of government, and the legislature met in a newly constructed Methodist church. Lucas concluded, however, that the only way to silence the jealous mutterings of the river towns would be to establish a permanent capital in a brand-new city farther inland.

Governor Lucas soon had other problems to contend with, when a boundary dispute flared between Iowa and Missouri. It started when Missouri tax collectors began knocking at the doors of southern Iowa cabins. The final insult came when a band of Missourians crossed the territory in question and chopped down three bee trees—hollow trees filled with wild honey. Honey was one of the few luxuries available to families on the frontier, and the Iowans were incensed. Governor Lucas called out the militia, and the Missouri governor did the same. A thousand angry Iowans, armed with pitchforks and squirrel rifles, marched south. But by the time they reached Farmington on the border, the Missouri militia had grown tired of waiting and had disbanded. The "Honey War" ended without a shot being fired. Eventually the border dispute was settled, in Iowa's favor.

The following year, three commissioners were appointed to choose the site for a new capital on a tract of "unoccupied public land" in Johnson County. The land was, in fact, occupied by about a thousand Sauk and Mesquakie. Once again, the Indians were forced to give up their homes. "Soon I shall go to a new home, and you will plant corn where my dead sleep," declared Chief Poweshiek as his people prepared to move yet again. "I know that I must go away, and you will be so glad when I am gone that you will soon forget that the meat and the lodge-fire of the Indian

An early photograph of Iowa's original state capitol in Iowa City

have been forever free to the stranger, and that at all times he has asked for what he fought for—the right to be free."

In 1841, the territorial legislature met for the first time in Iowa City, the new capital. At first, the business of government was conducted in a hotel; the great stone capitol building was not completed until 1851.

In the meantime, a swelling stream of land-hungry families poured into Iowa from states farther east. By 1844, some eighty thousand white settlers were living in Iowa. In 1846, one journalist wrote, "The roads [of Illinois and Indiana] would be literally lined with the long blue wagons of the immigrants, slowly wending their way over the broad prairies, often ten,

This 1853 photograph shows workers cutting down trees on what would become the grounds of the Iowa State Capitol in Des Moines.

twenty, and thirty wagons in the company. Ask them when and where you would, their destination was the Black Hawk Purchase—Iowa.''

Iowa asked to be admitted to the Union as a state in 1844, at a time when the question of slavery had begun to divide the nation. Southern congressmen protested that, if Iowa became a state, it would tip the balance in the legislature between slave and free states. In the final compromise, Iowa—the first free state west of the Mississippi River—entered the Union hand in hand with Florida—the last slave state east of the Mississippi. Slave and free states remained equally represented in Washington, D.C. On December 28, 1846, President James K. Polk signed the bill that made Iowa the twenty-ninth state to join the United States of America.

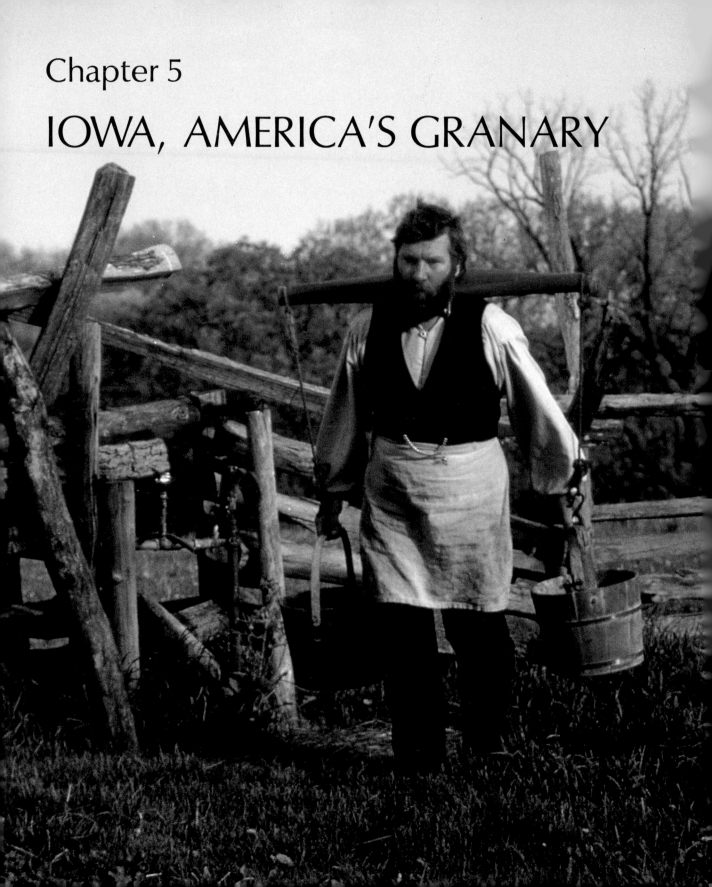

Chapter 5
IOWA, AMERICA'S GRANARY

IOWA, AMERICA'S GRANARY

THE WESTWARD MARCH

In New England and Pennsylvania, in Maryland and Virginia and Kentucky, in Ohio, Indiana, and Illinois, farmers dreamed of the rich black earth of the Iowa prairie. Soon all of the best land would be gobbled up, Iowa promoters warned them. Now was the time to hurry west!

Thousands of farmers heeded the warning. They sold their homes, loaded their furniture into wagons, and headed west with their wives, children, and livestock. Year by year, Iowa's population zoomed higher. By 1850, it had reached two hundred thousand. In the next decade, it soared to more than half a million.

As new towns sprang up across Iowa, dotting the prairie from the Mississippi to the Missouri, the amenities of civilization found their way to the frontier. Most communities supported a one-room school and supplemented its teacher's meager salary by providing room and board. The general store offered not only nails, molasses, and bolts of cloth, but a place for neighbors to gather and exchange news. Traveling ministers, or "circuit riders," went from town to town, preaching Sunday sermons in parlors or barns until proper churches could be built.

Loneliness and disease took a heavy toll on many frontier families. In her diary, one pioneer woman wrote, "I have had to pass through another season of sorrow. Death has again entered our home. This time it claimed our dear little John for its victim. It was hard for me to give him up, but dropsy on the brain ended its work in four short days. We are left again with one baby, and I feel that my health is giving way."

Although the church was often the center of the community, even the minister felt the hardships of frontier life. In 1842, twelve eager young Congregationalist pastors wrote to Asa Turner, a minister in the town of Denmark, explaining that they wanted to work in Iowa. "Don't come here expecting a paradise," Turner wrote back. "Come prepared to expect small things, rough things. . . . Get clothes, something firm and durable that will go through the hazel brush without tearing. Get wives of the old Puritan stamp, those who can milk a cow and churn the butter and be proud of a checked apron. . . . But it's no use to answer any more questions, for I never expect to see one of you west of the Mississippi River for as long as I live."

To Turner's surprise, eleven of the twelve pastors accepted the challenge and arrived in Iowa the following year. Known to history as the "Iowa Band," they founded churches across the state. They also established a college in Davenport that was later moved to Grinnell.

The year 1846 marks not only Iowa's statehood, but the beginning of the great Mormon migration to Utah. The Mormons, or members of the Church of Jesus Christ of Latter-day Saints, had founded the thriving town of Nauvoo in southern Illinois. But they were persecuted in Nauvoo, in part because they practiced polygamy—allowing a man to have several wives at once. After their founder, Joseph Smith, was killed by a mob, the Mormons crossed the Mississippi and set out on their long journey west in search of religious freedom.

Westward-bound Mormons holding a religious service at Council Bluffs

As they crossed southern Iowa, the first Mormon migrants set up a series of "Camps of Israel," where later bands could rest and gather supplies. Perhaps the most important of these camps was Mount Pisgah on the Grand River in Union County. Here the Mormons planted crops, erected a mill, and built a church, or tabernacle. For fourteen years, the wheels of Mormon wagons and oxcarts wore a deeply rutted trail for more than 300 miles (483 kilometers) across southern Iowa to Council Bluffs on the Missouri River.

BREAKING THE SOD

The Iowa promoters were right. When the first settlers reached the Black Hawk Purchase, they found a layer of rich topsoil 2 feet (0.6 meter) thick. However, before the land could be cultivated, it

Railroads first came to Iowa after Antoine LeClaire (above) persuaded the Chicago & Rock Island Railroad to build a bridge across the Mississippi between Davenport and Rock Island, Illinois (right).

had to be cleared and plowed. The open prairie presented a special set of problems. The roots of its dense wild grasses formed a nearly impenetrable mat that reached several inches below the earth's surface. Plows that had served well in Maryland or Ohio became hopelessly tangled when they assailed Iowa's prairie sod. Many farmers hired professional "prairie breakers," who used enormous plows pulled by several teams of oxen. A farmer might buy his land at only $1.25 per acre, but would then pay another $2.50 an acre to have the land prepared for the first planting.

Annoying as it was at plowing time, the tough sod had its uses. Blocks of sod, carved from the earth, proved an excellent building material on the treeless prairie. A house with sod walls 3 to 4 feet (0.9 to 1.2 meters) thick stayed warm in winter and cool during the summer.

Once furrows had been plowed and seed had been planted, the prairie yielded bumper crops of wheat, oats, and corn. In his autobiography *A Son of the Middle Border*, writer Hamlin Garland recalled the abundance of the fields his family tended: "Deep as the breast of a man, wide as the sea, heavy-headed, supple-stalked, many-voiced, . . . a meeting place of winds and of sunlight, our fields ran to the world's end."

From the beginning, farmers raised far more food than they could use themselves. But how could they ship their produce to the hungry markets back east?

Antoine LeClaire was a leading citizen in the town of Davenport, which he had helped to found after the Black Hawk Purchase. In 1853, LeClaire persuaded the Chicago & Rock Island Railroad to build a bridge across the Mississippi between Davenport and Rock Island, Illinois. LeClaire then organized the Mississippi & Missouri Railroad Company (the M & M), and launched his plan to extend the railroad line from Davenport through Iowa City and all the way to Council Bluffs.

Though they desperately needed a way to transport their produce, many Iowa farmers were suspicious of the project. Little by little, however, the railroad company won local support. After an agent addressed a meeting in Council Bluffs, one farmer stood up and declared, "My friends, I believe we should give this project a fair trial. I still have doubts about it, but, one of these days we will see the locomotive coming across the prairie with its head and tail up like a bedbug."

Once railroad-building got underway, Iowa City offered a reward if the line from Davenport arrived by New Year's Day, 1856. Tireless workmen, many of them recent immigrants from Ireland, labored day and night to complete the job. When the temperature plunged to minus 20 degrees Fahrenheit (minus 29

A locomotive at Fayette in 1872

degrees Celsius), huge bonfires were lighted along the right of
way to keep the men from freezing. At last, just before midnight
on December 31, 1855, the final spike was pounded in. The first
train, the *Antoine LeClaire*, roared into Iowa City to the
triumphant booming of cannons.

Despite this early success, the M & M did not reach Council
Bluffs until 1867. By that time, two other railroad companies
already had tracks spanning the state. A grid of spur lines joined
the main trunk lines. By 1880, every Iowan lived within 25 miles
(40 kilometers) of a railway depot.

The railroads brought eastern markets within easy reach of the
Iowa farmer. Iowa was on its way to becoming the granary of the

nation, a vast producer of grain for the country's hungry urban centers.

Not only did the trains carry Iowa produce east; they also sped manufactured goods from New England, New York, and Philadelphia westward to Iowa. Iowa was no longer a remote outpost on the frontier, but an integral part of a rapidly growing country.

As settlement spread toward the Missouri River, western Iowans argued that the state needed a centrally located capital that would be easily accessible to people from every region. In 1855, the General Assembly voted to move the seat of government from Iowa City west to Fort Des Moines, an army post at the Raccoon Fork of the Des Moines River.

THE INDIANS RETURN

By 1851, the last of Iowa's Native American people had been moved beyond the state's borders. The Sauk and Mesquakie had been resettled on reservation lands in Kansas, where they survived on regular annuity payments from the federal government. In 1857, a group of Mesquakie pooled their annuity money and bought 80 acres (32 hectares) of land along the Iowa River in Tama County. The government had paid them 10¢ an acre (4¢ a hectare) for their land in Iowa when they were forced to leave; to buy it back, they paid $12.50 per acre ($5.00 per hectare). At first, the government stopped sending annuity payments, claiming that the Mesquakie could receive federal help only if they remained on the Kansas reservation. For a few years, the Mesquakie eked out a meager existence, crowded onto a plot of land half the size of a typical Iowa farm today. Eventually, however, they managed to purchase some 3,000 acres

Today, Mesquakie Indians still own and reside on the piece of land in Tama County that they bought back from the federal government in the late 1850s.

(1,214 hectares) of land. This land is still held by the tribe today. Though it is commonly called the "Tama Indian Reservation," it is not truly a reservation, but private property, bought and paid for by the Mesquakie.

Like the Mesquakie, many of the Sioux missed their Iowa homeland. Even after they were officially relocated to Minnesota and the Dakotas, Sioux hunting parties occasionally crossed the Iowa border. During the savage winter of 1856-57, a chief named Inkpaduta and a group of Sioux warriors wandered into the northwestern corner of the state. Inkpaduta had been banished by the Sioux after he murdered his father. In Iowa, he and his followers begged for food from the white settlers and occasionally robbed isolated cabins.

In March 1857, Inkpaduta's group reached the cabin of Rowland Gardner near Spirit Lake in Dickinson County. The Sioux had

An 1895 photograph of the monument erected at the Gardner Cabin, site of the 1857 Spirit Lake massacre

long regarded Spirit Lake as sacred, and would not even paddle across it in a canoe. Now they found settlers' cabins scattered along its shores. Outraged, Inkpaduta attacked the Gardner family. He and his braves killed everyone in the cabin except fourteen-year-old Abbie Gardner, who was taken captive. Over the next several days, the Indians went swiftly from cabin to cabin around Spirit Lake and East and West Okoboji, murdering thirty-four men, women, and children.

The people of Iowa, who had been convinced that the "Indian problem" lay safely behind them, were appalled when they learned of the attacks. An expedition set out from Fort Dodge in pursuit of Inkpaduta, but became hindered by a series of blizzards. Inkpaduta escaped into the Dakota region and was never apprehended. After several months with the Sioux, Abbie Gardner and another captive were ransomed and returned to Iowa. Years later, Abbie Gardner wrote a vivid account of her terrifying experience in *History of the Spirit Lake Massacre.*

"AN INSEPARABLE UNION"

In 1839, Iowa's territorial supreme court had heard the case of a black man named Ralph. Ralph was a slave from Missouri who had been sent by his master to work in the lead mines at Dubuque. After he had lived in Iowa for two years, Ralph's master came from Missouri to take him home. But Ralph argued that he was no longer a slave, since for the past two years he had been living on free soil. The court ruled in Ralph's favor. Under Iowa law, he was a free man.

From its founding, Iowa had never permitted slavery within its borders. During the 1840s and 1850s, Iowans were gradually swept up in the nation's passionate debate over the slavery issue. Missouri, Iowa's neighbor to the south, had entered the Union as a slave state. Frequently, runaway slaves from Missouri fled into Iowa. Many headed north to Canada on the Underground Railroad, a secret network of safe houses, or "stations," where fugitives could find food and shelter. "Conductors" on the railroad transported runaways from one station to the next, often hiding them in wagons beneath bales of wheat or piles of corn. To aid an escaping slave violated federal law. The conductors and their families risked imprisonment in order to live by their belief that slavery was morally wrong.

One fugitive who made use of the Underground Railroad was not a runaway slave, but an ardent white abolitionist: John Brown. After his antislavery activities in Kansas got him into trouble with the law, Brown fled to Tabor, Iowa, and hid in the home of conductor John Todd. During the fall of 1857, Brown drilled a band of followers in Tabor's town park. Then, with a cache of two hundred rifles, he led his tiny army across Iowa to the Quaker settlement of Springdale.

The Todd House in Tabor (left), which served as a station on the Underground Railroad, once sheltered abolitionist John Brown (right).

Brown dreamed of sparking an uprising among southern blacks that would end slavery forever. He and his followers stayed in Springdale for several months, making secret plans. They then marched into Missouri, killed a slaveholder, and brought eleven slaves to Iowa. With still more Wanted notices offering a reward for his capture, Brown finally left the Hawkeye State.

Fired by Brown's ideals, Edwin and Barclay Coppoc, two Quaker brothers from Springdale, set out to join him. The Coppoc brothers were with Brown's band when it seized the arsenal at Harpers Ferry, Virginia, in October 1859. But no slave uprising ensued. Brown was hanged for treason, along with several of his men—among them Edwin Coppoc.

In 1860, Abraham Lincoln was elected president of the United States. Lincoln had run as the candidate of the antislavery Republican party, and news of his victory triggered panic in the southern states. One after another, they seceded from the Union, forming a new nation called the Confederate States of America.

A reenactment of a Civil War battle involving the 31st Iowa Regiment

When Confederate troops fired on Fort Sumter in Charleston, South Carolina, the nation plunged into a long and bloody civil war.

Some Iowa men enlisted in the Union army out of patriotic duty, or because they wanted to bring an end to slavery. But most, raised on farms or in quiet small towns, simply hungered for excitement. "I had gone into the army for adventure as well as patriotism," admitted Private S. H. M. Byers of Oskaloosa. "I was forever trying to get into the lines where the real adventures were going on. I foolishly wanted to see men killed in battle, and to take a real chance at being killed myself."

For the seventy thousand Iowans who served during the war years, the reality of military life was grim indeed. More than twelve thousand Iowans lost their lives, some eighty-five hundred of them dying not in battle, but of typhoid and other diseases that ravaged the camps.

Annie Wittenmyer, a widow from Keokuk, cared for the sick and wounded of both armies during the Civil War.

While the men endured forced marches, slim rations, and cannon fire, Iowa women, too, threw themselves into the war effort. Many nursed the wounded in makeshift camp hospitals. Annie Wittenmyer, a widow from Keokuk, established a hospital for the wounded of both armies after the fall of Vicksburg, Mississippi. She traveled throughout the country, setting up diet kitchens to ensure that sick and wounded soldiers would receive nourishing food. Mehitabel Woods of Fairfield transported more than 200 tons (180 metric tons) of food, medicines, and other supplies to Union troops on Confederate soil. When questioned, she would explain, "I am off to see my sons, who are all in the army."

In April 1865, Confederate General Robert E. Lee surrendered, and the war was over. The men and women of Iowa had upheld their state motto: "Our liberties we prize and our rights we will maintain."

PENNSYLVANIA

IOWA COMES OF AGE

The crowd cheered, and men tossed their hats into the air. William Morrison's electrically powered horseless carriage bounced and rumbled down the streets of Des Moines at a dizzying 20 miles (32 kilometers) per hour. Yet probably no one who watched that day in 1890 imagined that the horseless carriage—or automobile—would someday transform the American landscape.

Iowa has championed many inventions that changed everyday life in America. It also fostered innovations in the realms of agriculture and social programs as it moved into the twentieth century.

BUSINESS AND POLITICS

After the Civil War, Iowa passed a series of laws that made it a leader in civil-rights legislation. In 1868, an amendment to the state constitution extended the vote to black men. (Women, whether black or white, were not allowed to vote until 1920.) Another constitutional amendment, passed in 1880, permitted blacks to serve in the Iowa General Assembly. Several court decisions eliminated segregation in public schools. Mississippi steamboats had to be integrated as they passed through Iowa waters. President Ulysses S. Grant once called Iowa "the nation's one bright radical star."

The Republican party, which had emerged from the antislavery movement, remained the dominant political force in Iowa. During

In the late 1800's, William Boyd Allison (left) was Iowa's most powerful politician.

the late 1800s, a Republican congressman from Dubuque, William Boyd Allison, rose to become the most powerful man in the state.

Allison was elected to Congress for the first time in 1862, and served almost uninterrupted until his death in 1908. He was a soft-spoken man and was sometimes accused of being indecisive. But from his position in the House of Representatives, and later from the Senate, he carefully selected and promoted officials whom he could trust to carry out his policies in Iowa. Allison was a staunch believer in the rights and privileges of big business, including the railroad companies.

Iowa farmers could not survive without the railroads. The railroad companies often charged exorbitant rates for shipping produce, knowing that the farmers had no choice but to pay. After all the hard work of planting and weeding, after all the worries

The farmers' organization known as the Grange gained a large following in
Iowa in the late 1800s.

about grasshoppers and weather conditions, the farmers saw their
profits gobbled up at the train depots when they shipped their
crops to market.

The Grange, a farmers' organization that gained a large
following in Iowa, fought hard for laws that would regulate the
railroads. In the 1870s, Iowa finally passed a law that required a
state railroad commission to investigate unfair company practices.
But the commission was funded by the railroad companies
themselves, and the governor who appointed the commissioners
had virtually been chosen by William Boyd Allison.

In the gubernatorial election of 1886, Allison had thrown his
considerable political weight behind William Larrabee. Larrabee
was a mill owner who had voted against the railroad commission
bill. His speeches were long and dull, and not even Allison paid
much attention to what he said.

Newton became the washing-machine capital of the world after Fred Maytag introduced his first commercial washer (right) in 1907.

Once Larrabee was in office, however, Allison discovered he had made a disastrous mistake in supporting him. Larrabee had opposed the railroad law not because he favored the companies, but because he felt the commission would not be forceful enough. As governor, Larrabee called for immediate railroad reform. Though he mumbled his speeches, the people of Iowa heard his message. In 1888, the legislature passed the first effective railroad act in the state's history, creating a new commission with real power to fix fair rates for shipping.

Though Iowa remained a predominantly agricultural state, manufacturing grew in importance in the decades after the Civil War. In 1884, Fred Maytag of Newton invented a gas-powered machine that washed and wrung out clothes. Newton became the washing-machine capital of the world. Waterloo emerged as a major center for the production of tractors and other farm machinery. Meat packing became the key industry in Sioux City. Factories in Muscatine used a special process to turn the shells of freshwater mussels into shiny pearl buttons.

The locomotives that steamed across Iowa devoured coal. Railroad companies often operated mines in the coal belt that runs through the south-central part of the state. Around 1900, the Chicago & North Western Railroad brought in a group of black laborers from the southern states to break a miners' strike. The company settled the workers in Monroe County and created the mining community of Buxton. More than three thousand of Buxton's six thousand inhabitants were black. Black doctors, lawyers, teachers, and other professionals provided most of the services needed by the town. After 1918, the coal mines closed, and Buxton gradually dwindled into a ghost town.

DECADES OF TURMOIL

In 1917, the United States became embroiled in World War I, which had already been devastating Europe for three years. Farm prices boomed, and grain from Iowa's fields helped feed the hungry troops overseas. Unfortunately, one by-product of Iowa's patriotic zeal was a surge in anti-German feeling. Many German families had settled in the state during the nineteenth century, and German was still widely spoken in some communities. Governor William L. Harding decreed that only English could be used in public places, including churches, trains, and schools. German was not even permitted in telephone conversations. National headlines shouted with ridicule when five farm wives were arrested for speaking German over a party line.

During World War I, Herbert Hoover, a native of West Branch, earned worldwide acclaim when he organized a relief program for the people of beleaguered Belgium. After the war, Hoover served as United States secretary of commerce under two Republican presidents, Warren Harding and Calvin Coolidge. In 1928, he ran for office for the first time in his life, and was elected president of the United States.

Hoover entered the White House at an inopportune time. Throughout the 1920s, farm prices had been falling. Then, in 1929, a stock market crash in New York triggered a nationwide depression. Across the country, banks failed and factories laid off thousands of workers. When farm prices tumbled to an all-time low, farmers struggled for survival. People everywhere looked for someone to blame for their misfortunes. The accusing fingers pointed at President Hoover. All over the country, at the ragged edges of cities and towns, homeless people erected communities of tar-paper shacks. Such communities became known as "Hoovervilles."

In 1931, the state of Iowa launched a program to test dairy cattle for bovine tuberculosis, a disease that could be fatal to children who drank infected milk. Under the program, any cattle found to carry the disease would be destroyed. Already staggering under the hardships of the Great Depression, the farmers of Cedar and Muscatine counties picked up their guns and threatened to shoot any state veterinarian who came near their cows. Although Governor Dan Turner sympathized with the farmers, he was determined to see the law enforced. He called out troops, and the testing was completed under armed guard. History remembers this incident as the "Cow War."

In the summer of 1932, a group of Iowa farmers attempted to fight low prices by holding all produce off the market for at least a week. In an effort to launch the strike, they blockaded the roads into Sioux City and prevented farmers from bringing their

In 1931, in what became known as the "Cow War," the testing of Iowa cattle for bovine tuberculosis was carried out under armed guard.

produce into town. One man was shot and killed as he tried to pass through the blockade. Few farmers cooperated with the strike, however, and it was finally called off.

In the presidential election of 1932, Iowa broke its time-honored Republican tradition and voted overwhelmingly for the Democratic candidate, Franklin D. Roosevelt. When forming his cabinet, Roosevelt selected Iowan Henry A. Wallace as secretary of agriculture. While serving in this position, from 1933 to 1940, Wallace developed many of the "New Deal" policies that aided farmers in Iowa and throughout the country. He promoted soil conservation and the standardization of prices for produce. Wallace also upheld the controversial notion that the government should maintain higher prices by paying some farmers *not* to grow crops. As vice-president under Roosevelt, from 1940 to 1944, Wallace continued to shape the nation's agricultural policy.

Iowa and the nation finally emerged from the Great Depression only to face another hurdle—World War II. Once again, farm

Soviet Premier Nikita Khrushchev visited an Iowa farm during his 1959 trip to the United States.

prices boomed. Iowa corn helped to feed thousands of American servicemen at home and abroad.

The United States plunged into the war after the Japanese bombed Pearl Harbor, in Hawaii, on December 7, 1941. Just weeks later, five young men, the Sullivan brothers of Waterloo, walked into a naval recruiting office. They were eager to avenge the death of their friend, Bill Ball of Fredericksburg, who had died in the attack. The Sullivan brothers, insisting that they stay together, were assigned to the light cruiser USS *Juneau*. In 1942, all five lost their lives when the ship was sunk off Guadalcanal. Not since the Civil War had one family lost so many sons in a single battle.

The Sullivan brothers became a symbol of American courage and patriotism during World War II. A warship was even named in their honor. Among the heartfelt letters of condolence that poured in for the bereaved family was a note from the First Lady.

"I shall keep the memory of your fortitude always in mind, as I hope other mothers with sons in the service will do," wrote Eleanor Roosevelt. "It is heartening that parents who have suffered the loss you have can always find solace in your faith and your abiding love for our country."

CHANGES AND CHALLENGES

One morning in 1959, a squadron of Secret Service men and reporters descended on a farm near Coon Rapids. The focus of the excitement was Soviet Premier Nikita Khrushchev, who had come to visit a typical Iowa farm. "Khrushchev came for symbolic reasons, to show the Russian people his interest in agriculture," farmer Roswell Garst recalled years later. "He was a real man. He knew how to laugh and yell. So we laughed and yelled back and forth for three or four hours. I enjoyed it, frankly."

By the time of Khrushchev's visit, Iowa's agriculture was famous throughout the world. The homesteaders of a century before would scarcely have recognized the patchwork of neatly fenced fields. They would have marveled at the shiny gasoline-powered tractors that effortlessly cut rows of straight, clean furrows. Most of the swaying cornstalks were hybrid plants, carefully bred for high yield and resistance to insect pests. Iowa farmers had turned agriculture into a science.

Farming had changed in other ways, as well. As technology made raising crops more efficient, fewer hands could work larger plots of land. Fewer children followed the farming tradition of their fathers and grandfathers. More and more young people moved to the towns to take jobs in shops and offices. In 1960, the federal census showed that urban dwellers outnumbered rural citizens for the first time in Iowa's history.

Many people not only abandoned the farm, but left Iowa altogether. During the 1950s and 1960s, Iowa's population growth slowed. The state saw a brief upswing during the 1970s, but in the 1980s, population figures dipped once more.

By the 1980s, farmers could demand higher prices than ever before for their produce. But soaring expenses devoured their growing profits. In 1981, the *Des Moines Register* pointed out that the average farmer's net income (the money he could keep, after paying expenses) had actually dropped 76 percent since 1973. Many farmers borrowed heavily and found themselves hopelessly in debt. By 1984, one of every three Iowa farmers had serious financial problems.

To make matters worse, nature seemed to turn against the farmer. A disastrous drought in 1988 parched fields and dried up wells and ponds. Moreover, agricultural experts warned that wind and water erosion were carrying away Iowa's precious topsoil year by year. The homesteaders of the 1800s had found a layer of tillable soil 2 feet (0.6 meter) thick. On average, only 8 inches (20 centimeters) of topsoil remained in most parts of the state by 1990.

While farm families were leaving the land, Iowa began to attract a new breed of immigrants. The newcomers were well-educated professionals—doctors, teachers, researchers—lured not by Iowa's black earth but by its good schools, scenic villages, and low crime rate. In Iowa they found a sense of community that was missing in such crowded, bustling cities as Chicago and St. Louis. Overall, however, about two hundred thousand more people left Iowa than moved into the state during the 1980s. Many of those who packed up and moved away were recent college graduates, eager to find jobs and adventure in the world beyond the Hawkeye State.

An Iowa farmer watering his sheep during the devastating drought of 1988

In 1990, Michael Gartner of the *Daily Tribune* of Ames
published an open letter in the *Wall Street Journal*. The letter was
addressed to Dr. Louis Sullivan, secretary of health and human
services, who had been invited to deliver the commencement
speech at Simpson College. But in effect, Gartner spoke to all
Iowans, especially the state's young people. "Please urge these
youths to stay in Iowa," Gartner wrote. "Tell them the world is an
exciting place, and urge them to see it. . . . But tell them, please,
that they are Iowans, that they are needed in the hometown, or at
least the home state, that there are opportunities here and that
they can make others of their own, and that, in fact, this is the
place many in the rest of the world are looking for—a pretty place
with clean air and clear values, with natural resources and
unnatural harmony."

Chapter 7

GOVERNMENT AND THE ECONOMY

GOVERNMENT AND THE ECONOMY

GOVERNMENT

Iowa's state constitution was ratified in 1857 and has been amended about forty times. Amendments, or changes, may come from the legislature or from a constitutional convention called for by the voters. The constitution divides Iowa's state government into three main branches: legislative, judicial, and executive. The legislative branch passes or repeals laws; the judicial branch interprets the laws; and the executive branch ensures that the laws are carried out.

The Iowa legislature, known as the general assembly, consists of two houses. The upper house, or senate, has fifty members who are elected to four-year terms. The one hundred members of the lower house, or house of representatives, are elected to two-year terms. Regular sessions of the general assembly begin each year on the second Monday in January.

Iowa is divided into eight judicial districts, each served by a district court. Cases from the district courts may be sent on to the statewide court of appeals. At the top of Iowa's judicial system is the state supreme court in Des Moines. Iowa's nine supreme court justices are appointed by the governor, but must later be approved by the voters.

The governor, or chief executive, may be elected to an unlimited number of four-year terms. In addition to appointing supreme court justices, the governor selects the officers of about twenty state agencies and departments. The governor has the power to

An interior view
of the Iowa State
Capitol dome

veto laws passed by the legislature. But this veto can be overruled
by a two-thirds vote in both the house and the senate.

About 60 percent of the money in Iowa's state budget comes
from taxes. Iowans pay a general sales tax and special taxes on
insurance, tobacco, and gasoline. Personal and corporate income
taxes provide a key portion of state revenue. In addition, Iowa
receives millions of dollars through federal grants and programs.

EDUCATION

The most expensive item in Iowa's state budget is education.
Iowa has placed a high value on learning since the pioneer days.
In 1830, Dr. Isaac Galland started the first school in the Iowa

Iowa's many fine institutions of higher learning include Cornell College (left) and Drake University (right).

Territory in a one-room cabin near present-day Galland. According to legend, the only pay the teacher received was permission to read the doctor's medical books. Today, all Iowa children between the ages of seven and sixteen must attend school.

Iowa is home to more than thirty fully accredited colleges and universities. The University of Iowa at Iowa City, which opened in 1857, trains students for careers in business administration, education, engineering, law, medicine, nursing, art, library science, social work, and many other professional fields. Iowa State University was founded at Ames in 1858 as the Iowa State Agricultural College and Model Farm. Today, Iowa State's colleges include schools of agriculture, veterinary medicine, engineering, and home economics. Iowa State Teachers College, founded in 1876 in an abandoned orphanage in Cedar Falls, evolved into the University of Northern Iowa.

Barges on the Mississippi River near Marquette

One of Iowa's most unusual institutions of higher learning is the Palmer College of Chiropractic Medicine in Davenport, which teaches a sometimes controversial method of healing by manipulating the spinal column. Among Iowa's other colleges are Coe College, in Cedar Rapids; Cornell College, in Mount Vernon; Drake University, in Des Moines; Grinnell College, in Grinnell; Luther College, in Decorah; Simpson College, in Indianola; and William Penn College, in Oskaloosa.

TRANSPORTATION AND COMMUNICATION

Cars, trucks, and buses cross Iowa on some 112,000 miles (180,242 kilometers) of paved roads and highways. Six railway lines operate freight trains on 4,700 miles (7,564 kilometers) of track. Iowa has about 355 airports, the largest of which are in Des Moines, Cedar Rapids, Dubuque, Sioux City, and Waterloo. Mississippi River barges load and unload at Dubuque, Davenport,

Hay (above) is one of the many crops produced in Iowa.

and Keokuk. In 1964, the Army Corps of Engineers dredged portions of the Missouri River, making it navigable by cargo ships all the way to Sioux City.

Iowa's first newspaper, the *Du Buque Visitor*, appeared in 1836. Today, the most widely read paper in the state is the highly acclaimed *Des Moines Register*. Other leading newspapers include the *Cedar Rapids Gazette*, the *Sioux City Journal*, the *Telegraph-Herald* of Dubuque, the *Waterloo Courier*, and the *Quad City Times*, published in Davenport.

Iowa's first radio station, WSUI, began broadcasting at the University of Iowa in 1919. WOC of Davenport, the state's first commercial station, went on the air in 1922. WOC was owned by B. J. Palmer of the Palmer Institute, who used the station to spread the word about the benefits of chiropractic treatment. In 1949, Iowans saw their first television programs when WOC-TV began

Corn (left) and hogs (above) are
Iowa's leading agricultural products.

operating in Davenport. Today Iowa has about 180 AM and FM
radio stations and 15 television stations.

AGRICULTURE

About 93 percent of Iowa's land is devoted to agriculture. The
state's 111,000 farms average about 320 acres (130 hectares) in
size. Iowa provides about 7 percent of the nation's food, and, in
addition, sends much of its grain overseas. Nevertheless,
agriculture constitutes only about 7 percent of Iowa's gross state
product (GSP) — the total value of all goods and services produced
in the state during a given year.

Corn is the leading source of farm income in Iowa. Year by
year, Iowa vies with Illinois for the position of number-one corn
producer in the nation. Much of Iowa's corn is used as feed for

livestock. Iowa ranks second among the states (behind Illinois) in soybean production. Other field crops include oats, rye, alfalfa, wheat, and flaxseed.

Apples are Iowa's leading fruit crop. The Red Delicious apple was developed in the 1880s by Jesse Hiatt on a farm near Winterset. Iowa may run neck and neck with Illinois in corn production, but it is the unchallenged leader among the states in raising hogs. Iowa farms produce about 14 million hogs per year—accounting for one-third of the nation's pork, ham, and bacon. Iowa is also a leading producer of beef. Dairy cows graze in the hilly northeastern corner of the state. Farms throughout the state produce chickens and eggs.

MANUFACTURING

Manufacturing comprises about one-fifth of Iowa's GSP. Most of the manufactured goods made in the state are directly related to farming or farm products. Tractors and other farm machinery are assembled at plants in Dubuque, Davenport, Des Moines, and Waterloo.

Food processing is another Iowa industry closely connected to Iowa agriculture. Major meat-packing plants operate in Sioux City, and the Quaker Oats plant in Cedar Rapids is one of the largest cereal mills in the world. Not surprisingly, Iowa is a leading producer of corn products, including cornstarch, corn oil, and corn sugar. The nation's largest popcorn-processing plant is located in Sioux City.

Newton is still known for the manufacture of washing machines. Other goods from Iowa factories include chemicals, fabricated metal products, printed materials, and rubber and plastic products.

The Quaker Oats plant in Cedar Rapids is one of the world's largest cereal mills.

SERVICE INDUSTRIES

Service industries account for more than two-thirds of Iowa's GSP. Instead of producing goods for sale, workers in the service industries offer services to groups or individuals. In Iowa, retail and wholesale trade employ more people than any other industry. The wholesale trade of farm equipment and farm products is a vital aspect of the state's economy. Cedar Rapids, Davenport, Des Moines, Sioux City, and Waterloo all serve as major trading centers for agricultural goods. Many Iowans are employed in the shipping of farm products by truck or rail.

Iowa's finance, insurance, and real estate industries are most heavily concentrated in and around Des Moines. The headquarters of more than fifty insurance companies are located in Des Moines, sometimes called the "Hartford of the West."

75

Chapter 8
ARTS AND RECREATION

ARTS AND RECREATION

In the late nineteenth century, the high point of the year in Iowa's small towns was the Chautauqua. A ten-day extravaganza of visiting lecturers, musicians, and theater troupes, the Chautauqua helped quench the peoples' thirst for culture and entertainment.

Today, though television and the VCR have replaced the Chautauqua, Iowans remain committed to the arts. The Hawkeye State has given the nation some of its most outstanding writers, painters, and musicians. In addition, the state has produced many fine athletes, and sponsors sporting events that delight native Iowans and visitors of all ages.

LITERATURE

Probably the first Iowan to write a full-length book was Sauk Chief Black Hawk. Shortly before his death in 1838, Black Hawk dictated his autobiography to Antoine LeClaire, the founder of Davenport. Iowa's early days are also documented in a vast storehouse of homesteaders' letters and diaries that have been collected at the State Historical Society of Iowa in Iowa City and Des Moines.

The first Iowa writer to win enduring national recognition was Hamlin Garland, whose work drew heavily from his childhood on

Black Hawk (left) and Hamlin Garland (above) both wrote autobiographies that detailed their experiences in Iowa.

the Iowa frontier. Born in Wisconsin in 1860, Garland moved to Iowa with his family when he was a young boy, and grew up on a farm near Osage. His stories in *Main-Travelled Roads*, *Prairie Folk*, and *Wayside Courtships* reveal the cruel hardships of pioneer life. His 1917 autobiography, *A Son of the Middle Border*, is a vivid recollection of his family's homesteading years. Garland's bitter realism was often shocking to his readers, who expected literature to deal with heroism and romance instead of hunger, disease, and loneliness.

The novels of Herbert Quick, who grew up in Grundy County, also reflect a frontier upbringing. After working as a teacher and a lawyer, Quick turned to writing. In a series of three interconnected novels, *Vandemark's Folly*, *The Hawkeye*, and *The Invisible Woman*, he traces Iowa's early history.

Bess Streeter Aldrich, of Cedar Falls, is best remembered for her 1928 novel of pioneer life, *A Lantern in Her Hand*. Another Iowa writer who achieved success in the 1920s and 1930s was Ruth Suckow, author of *Country People, Iowa Interiors*, and *The Folks*.

Novelist Edna Ferber spent seven years of her childhood in the town of Ottumwa, where her father ran an unsuccessful business. She later claimed that her exposure to life on the Des Moines and Mississippi rivers helped inspire her bestseller *Show Boat*, which was eventually made into a popular musical.

During the second half of the twentieth century, literary life in the Hawkeye State centered around the Writers' Workshop at the University of Iowa in Iowa City. This prestigious two-year workshop—considered the most respected writing program in the nation—has attracted many of America's leading contemporary writers of prose and poetry. Among the illustrious men and women who have spent time at the workshop, either as students or teachers or both, are Flannery O'Connor, Tennessee Williams, Kurt Vonnegut, Jr., William Stafford, Raymond Carver, Gail Godwin, John Irving, and John Cheever.

ART

Nineteenth-century artist George Catlin is best known for his paintings of Indian life in the far West. Much of his work, however, depicts Indians as they lived in Iowa before the coming of white settlers. Among Catlin's best-known pictures are a portrait of Sauk Chief Keokuk and a vivid painting of the Sioux Bear Dance.

John James Audubon also visited Iowa when the prairie was still nearly untouched. Several of the famous pictures in his collection *Birds of America* were painted on a Potawatomi Indian

Keokuk on Horseback, **by George Catlin**

reservation that existed briefly in the southwestern corner of the state.

Native Americans were the subjects of two of Iowa's leading sculptors. Sherry Edmundson Fry's bronze statue of Iowa Chief Mahaska stands in the city square in Oskaloosa. Nellie Verne Walker is remembered for her statue of Keokuk, which she completed in 1913. Another sculptor, Vinnie Ream Hoxie, best known for the marble statue of Abraham Lincoln that stands in the U.S. Capitol, spent several summers in Iowa during the 1880s. She created statues of two of Iowa's leading figures of the Civil War period—Governor Samuel Kirkwood and Senator James Harlan.

The artistic achievements of Grant Wood rank him among the nation's most celebrated painters. Wood grew up on a farm near

The stained-glass window that Grant Wood designed for the Cedar Rapids American Legion Hall is today displayed in the lobby of the Veteran's Memorial Building in the heart of the city.

Anamosa, and later taught art in the public schools of Cedar Rapids. In 1927, Wood received his first paid assignment—a stained-glass window for the Cedar Rapids American Legion building. A meticulous craftsman, Wood went to Germany to learn the best techniques for working with stained glass. When the window was completed, however, its design was so unusual that the American Legion refused to accept it.

Wood received wide recognition in 1930, when his painting *American Gothic* was exhibited in Chicago. This painting—one of America's most recognizable—shows a father and daughter standing before a plain nineteenth-century Iowa farmhouse. *American Gothic* and many of Wood's later paintings offer a starkly realistic vision of rural life on the prairie. Wood spent the last years of his life teaching art at the University of Iowa in Iowa City.

Grant Wood's sister, a Cedar Rapids doctor, and this Eldon farmhouse (above) served as the models for Wood's famous painting *American Gothic* (left).

PERFORMING ARTS

Theater, dance, and music flourish in the Hawkeye State. The state's many colleges and universities sponsor a wealth of concerts and plays. The Cedar Rapids Symphony Orchestra presents concerts at the Paramount Theater for the Performing Arts. Cedar Rapids also hosts a community theater and a children's theater. The state capital is home to the Des Moines Symphony Orchestra, Des Moines Community Playhouse, and Des Moines Civic Ballet.

For a few days each summer, Davenport swings with a special beat as thousands of jazz fans from all over the country flock to the Bix Beiderbecke Jazz Festival. Leon Bismarck "Bix" Beiderbecke was born in Davenport in 1903, and began playing

Girls' high-school basketball (left) and rodeos (right) are among the sports that draw enthusiastic crowds in Iowa.

jazz cornet on Mississippi River showboats when he was sixteen. One of his tutors was trumpet-player Louis Armstrong. A genius at improvisation, Beiderbecke composed such jazz classics as ''In a Mist,'' ''Candlelight,'' and ''Davenport Blues.'' Tragically, he slid into alcoholism and died at the age of twenty-eight. After Beiderbecke's death, Louis Armstrong remarked, ''If that boy had lived, he'd be the greatest.''

SPORTS

Both as fans and as participants, Iowans enjoy a lively world of sports. High-school basketball and football are followed with wild enthusiasm. Girls' basketball at the high-school level enjoys enormous support in the Hawkeye State. One of the nation's premier track meets is the Drake Relays, sponsored by Drake University in Des Moines. Every August, balloonists from all over

Indianola hosts the annual National Hot Air Balloon Championship.

the country flock to Indianola to participate in the National Hot Air Balloon Championship. The annual Tri-State Rodeo draws crowds to Fort Madison in September.

With no major professional teams competing in Iowa, fan loyalty is channeled to the University of Iowa, whose teams play in the rugged Big Ten Conference. Twice during the 1980s, the Iowa Hawkeye football team fought its way to the coveted Rose Bowl, only to lose to Pacific Ten squads. In basketball, too, the University of Iowa has fielded strong teams.

Iowa has produced many famous baseball players. Most noteworthy is Bob Feller, who was born in Van Meter. Feared for his dazzling fastball, Feller pitched five no-hitters for Van Meter high school in 1936. He went on to star in the 1940s and 1950s with the Cleveland Indians. One of baseball's greatest old-time players was Cap Anson, who was born in Marshalltown and played for the Philadelphia Athletics in the 1800s. Anson's father, Henry Anson, was an Iowa pioneer who founded Marshalltown.

Chapter 9

A QUICK TOUR OF THE HAWKEYE STATE

A QUICK TOUR OF THE HAWKEYE STATE

Oh, there's nothing halfway about the Iowa way
we treat you,
When we treat you, which we may not do at all.
There's an Iowa kind, a special
chip-on-the-shoulder attitude
We've never been without that we recall. . . .

But we'll give you our shirt,
And our back to go with it,
If your crops should happen to die,
So what the heck, you're welcome,
Glad to have you with us,
Even though we may not ever mention it again—
You really ought to give Iowa a try!

In his Broadway hit *The Music Man*, Meredith Willson gently poked fun at the Iowa character. To understand Iowa's unique blend of friendliness and reserve, conservatism and openness to new ideas, it is necessary to pay a visit to the Hawkeye State.

WESTERN IOWA

Along the mighty Missouri River, the land rises in a series of scenic bluffs. The city of Council Bluffs was named for one such lofty cliff across the river from where Lewis and Clark held a meeting with a group of Oto Indians. One of the city's most important historic sites is the General Dodge House, the fully restored home of Grenville M. Dodge, a Civil War general and construction engineer for the Union Pacific Railroad. The

The interior of the General Dodge House in Council Bluffs

Mormon Trail Monument in Bayliss Park marks the point where the Mormons crossed into Nebraska at the end of their long trek across Iowa.

One of the most unusual attractions in Council Bluffs is the Squirrel Cage Jail. Wedge-shaped cells in this "lazy Susan" jail are arranged within a three-story rotating drum. The jail was ingeniously designed to prevent escape, as the cells themselves have no doors. A hand-operated crank enabled the jailer to turn the entire structure, bringing any cell in line with the single doorway. The Squirrel Cage Jail remained in use in Pottawattamie County until 1969.

The Todd House in Tabor served as a station on the Underground Railroad and once sheltered radical abolitionist John Brown. The unassuming frame house has been restored to look as it did in the turbulent years before the Civil War.

Elk Horn's Danish Windmill (left) and the Squirrel Cage Jail in Council
Bluffs (right) are two popular western Iowa attractions.

History comes alive for visitors at the Nishna Heritage Museum
in Oakland, once a small-town general store. Oakland's main
street has been refurbished to display the elegance of its late-
nineteenth-century architecture.

Northeast of Oakland lie the Danish-American communities of
Elk Horn and Kimballton. In 1976, the people of Elk Horn
transported a windmill from Denmark piece by piece, complete
with its 2,000-pound (907-kilogram) grindstone. The mill's 30,000
numbered parts were reassembled in Elk Horn, where its huge
blades now turn proudly in the wind. Kimballton celebrates its
Danish heritage as well. In the town square stands a replica of the
famous statue of the Little Mermaid from Hans Christian
Andersen's beloved fairy tale of the same name.

Lewis and Clark State Park, west of Onawa, marks a spot where
the explorers spent several days in the summer of 1804, observing

The K. D. Stockyards Station in Sioux City

the local flora and fauna. The park offers skiing, picnicking, and camping facilities, as well as boating on Blue Lake.

Sioux City's history as a leading meat-packing center is remembered at the K. D. Stockyards Station. This massive old brick building now serves as a shopping mall filled with restaurants, specialty shops, and even a bowling alley. The Sioux City Public Museum, housed in a Romanesque mansion, displays an outstanding collection of Indian artifacts, military memorabilia, period costumes, and specimens of plants and animals. On a high bluff overlooking the Missouri River stands a stone memorial to Sergeant Charles Floyd of the Lewis and Clark Expedition, the first United States soldier buried in Iowa.

Every summer, Storm Lake becomes a vacation playground, with swimming, boating, and fishing. In Albert City, north of the

The Legends of Rock and Roll Monument, in Clear Lake, honors rock legends Buddy Holly, Richie Valens, and the Big Bopper, who died in a plane crash after performing in Clear Lake in 1959.

lake, stands the old Chicago, Milwaukee & Pacific Railroad Depot, now on the National Register of Historic Places.

The region known as the Iowa Great Lakes lies in western Iowa along the Minnesota border. This area was the site of the tragic Spirit Lake Massacre of 1857. The Spirit Lake Massacre Monument, on West Okoboji Lake, is dedicated to the people who perished during the raids. The home of Abbie Gardner, who survived capture and later wrote about her experiences, still stands in Arnolds Park.

CENTRAL IOWA

The town of River City, Iowa, immortalized in Meredith Willson's Broadway hit *The Music Man*, was modeled on the

Ornamental rocks and gems from all over the world have been incorporated into the Grotto of the Redemption, in West Bend.

author's hometown of Mason City. Every June, Mason City hosts the North Iowa Band Festival. It is an event that would thrill Willson's Professor Harold Hill, who assured the boys of River City that they could become virtuosos if they would only think hard enough about their instruments.

Each year, devotees of the music of the 1950s pay their respects at the Legends of Rock and Roll Monument in Clear Lake. The monument honors rock legends Buddy Holly, Richie Valens, and J. D. Richardson (better known as the "Big Bopper"), who died in a plane crash after performing at Clear Lake in 1959.

Begun in 1912, the Grotto of the Redemption in West Bend was the life's work of Father Paul Dobberstein. Father Dobberstein spent years gathering gems from around the world and setting them in a series of nine rock grottos, each depicting a scene from the life of Christ. The precious stones in the grottos are estimated to have a value of $2.5 million.

Iowa State University in Ames

Southeast of West Bend is the town of Fort Dodge. The Fort Museum commemorates Fort Dodge's origins as a military post to protect early settlers from the Sioux. A reconstructed frontier village on the museum grounds includes a one-room school, jail, blacksmith shop, and general store. The Blanden Memorial Art Gallery features nineteenth- and twentieth-century works by American and European artists, as well as Asian decorative arts from the 1600s. In 1856, Fort Dodge competed with the town of Homer to become the seat of Webster County. According to legend, the question was finally settled by a wrestling match. The challenger from Fort Dodge won.

Beautiful Dolliver State Park, on the Des Moines River just northwest of Lehigh, is noted for its impressive cliffs and maze of limestone caves. Several works by Mound Builders lie within the park, including the famous Woman Mound. Nearby, Brushy Creek State Park offers hiking and bridle trails and 175 campsites.

The Des Moines Botanical Center houses some fifteen thousand varieties of plants.

Probably the most celebrated native of Moingona, just southwest of Boone, was Kate Shelley. On the stormy night of July 6, 1881, fifteen-year-old Kate noticed that the railroad bridge over Honey Creek had been swept away. Clutching a lantern, she crawled across a swaying bridge over the Des Moines River and warned the station agent. The agent stopped an oncoming passenger train, and hundreds of lives were saved. Kate's heroism is honored at Moingona's Kate Shelley Park and Railroad Museum.

The town of Ames grew up around Iowa State University, Iowa's outstanding college of agricultural sciences. The 110-foot (34-meter) brick tower of the Campanile presides over the campus. The Campanile houses a magnificent carillon of thirty-six bells, whose chimes ring clearly throughout the town.

Des Moines is Iowa's capital, cultural center, and largest city. The majestic gilded dome of the Iowa State Capitol is a cherished

Terrace Hill is the official home of the state governor.

Iowa landmark. On display in the capitol are a scale model of the World War II battleship *Iowa* and a collection of dolls representing the state's First Ladies in their inaugural gowns.

One of Des Moines' many outstanding historic houses is Terrace Hill, now the official home of the governor. Other historic dwellings include the forty-three-room Salisbury House and the simpler fourteen-room Jordan House, which was once a station on the Underground Railroad.

The Iowa State Historical Building is a four-story treasure trove of fossils, Indian artifacts, letters, photographs, antique toys, and other objects, all of which document the state's development. Visitors gain a unique perspective on the past at the Living History Farms—three fully operating farms that demonstrate the agricultural methods of 1840, 1900, and the future.

Agricultural methods of the past are demonstrated at the Living History Farms in Des Moines.

An authentically restored Dutch pioneer home in Pella

Movie buffs revere the town of Winterset as the birthplace of the "Duke"—that strong, silent man of action, John Wayne. Portions of Wayne's house have been restored to look as they did in 1907, the year the actor was born. The house also contains a museum displaying memorabilia from the actor's long career.

In 1848, immigrants from the Netherlands founded the town of Pella. Pella's Dutch heritage comes to life at the Historical Village Museum, a reconstructed Dutch frontier community complete with general store, potter's shop, smithy, several cabins, and a gristmill. Pella was the boyhood home of Wyatt Earp, one of the legendary tamers of the Wild West.

Formed by a 2-mile (3-kilometer) dam, Rathbun Lake, in south-central Iowa, is the state's largest body of water. The lake lies within a sprawling state park that is a haven for hikers and bird-watchers.

The stately Old Capitol, in Iowa City, is Iowa's most historic building.

EASTERN IOWA

Iowa City served as Iowa's capital from 1839 until 1857. The stately Old Capitol is now a museum. Plum Grove, the fully restored home of Territorial Governor Robert Lucas, is sometimes referred to as Iowa's Mount Vernon.

The University of Iowa provides a wealth of cultural opportunities for the people of Iowa City. Dozens of concerts, plays, and lectures are open to the public throughout the school year. In addition, the university maintains an excellent museum of art, and a museum of natural history with a special collection of mounted North American birds.

West Branch was the birthplace of Herbert Hoover, the first American president born west of the Mississippi River. The house where Hoover was born stands within a 197-acre (80-hectare) park. Hoover and his wife are both buried on a hillside within the

Visitors can buy beautifully crafted items at a number of shops in Amana (left), including the well-known Amana Woolen Mill (right).

park grounds. Historians from all over the country come to West Branch to do research at the Hoover Presidential Library and Museum.

The Amana Colonies are a cluster of seven villages founded by the Community of True Inspiration, a German Protestant sect. From the 1850s until 1932, the villages operated under a communal system of government, with all residents sharing equally in the property and the work. Although the villagers finally shifted to a private enterprise economy, Amana has not lost its respect for the past or its sense of community.

The Museum of Amana History is a complex of three buildings, including a restored 1864 home and a schoolhouse used from 1870 to 1955. The century-old Amana Woolen Mill is a fine place to buy high-quality blankets and tartan plaid capes and sweaters. Other shops sell such handmade items as candles, baskets, and

The Cedar Rapids Museum of Art is renowned for its collection of works by Grant Wood.

furniture, and feature demonstrations of craftspeople at their work. The Amana villages are dotted with restaurants that offer delectable country-style meals.

On the Cedar River, northeast of the Amana Colonies, stands Cedar Rapids, one of Iowa's largest cities. The Cedar Rapids Museum of Art boasts the world's biggest collection of works by renowned Iowa painter Grant Wood. The stained-glass window that Wood designed for the Cedar Rapids American Legion Hall is on display in the lobby of the Veterans Memorial Building in the heart of the city.

For many years, Cedar Rapids had the highest percentage of Czechs of any city in the nation. The city's Czech heritage lives on at the Czech Village and Czech Museum. The Czech Village is famous for its tempting bakeries and Old World-style markets. The museum's exhibits include a collection of exquisite antique costumes from Czechoslovakia.

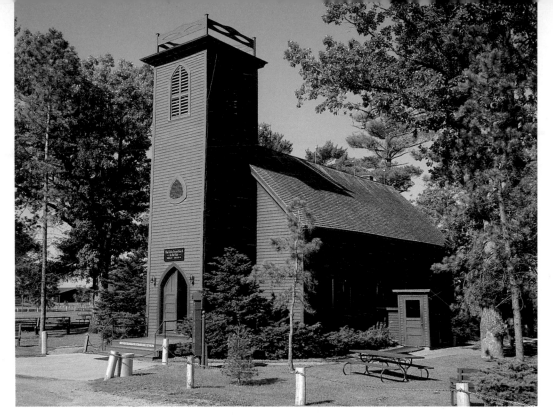

The Little Brown Church, in Nashua, is a popular wedding chapel.

Intrepid travelers can make a 52-mile (84-kilometer) journey from Hiawatha, just north of Cedar Rapids, to Evansdale, outside Waterloo, by hiking the Cedar Valley Nature Trail. Following the old Illinois Central Gulf Railroad line, the trail hugs the Cedar River as it meanders through scenic parklands and passes charming small towns.

Exhibits at Waterloo's Grout Museum of History and Science run the gamut from specimens of local minerals to Civil War relics and antique musical instruments. The Ice House Museum, in nearby Cedar Falls, demonstrates how Iowa pioneers once harvested and stored blocks of river ice—their only means of refrigeration.

Waverly, just north of Waterloo, is home to the slightly offbeat Schield International Museum. The museum houses the private collection of a millionaire machinery manufacturer who gathered unusual objects from all over the world. Exhibits range from Persian rugs to elephant tusks.

Every year, couples from all over the country arrange to be married at the Little Brown Church in Nashua. Built in 1864, the church stands on the site that inspired the beloved hymn "The Church in the Wildwood."

During the summer of 1893, Czech composer Antonín Dvořák lived and worked in the town of Spillville. Today, the house where Dvořák lived serves as the Bily Clock Museum, displaying a rare collection of hand-carved clocks.

Northwest of Cresco spreads the 240-acre (97-hectare) Hayden Prairie, its tall grasses sprinkled with wildflowers like those that greeted Iowa's first white settlers. During the 1940s, Ada Hayden, a botany professor from Iowa State University, fought relentlessly to save examples of Iowa's vanishing prairie ecosystem. In one eloquent speech, she told her audience that the prairie lands would be "a preserve for your grandchildren and great-grand-children to enjoy—not as a picnic ground, but as a cathedral, a monument to the past." The Hayden Prairie is the largest of some sixty tracts of original prairie that survive in Iowa.

DOWN THE MISSISSIPPI

On the bluffs overlooking the Mississippi River, some 191 ancient burial mounds are preserved at Effigy Mounds National Monument, just north of Marquette. These mounds, some of which are shaped like animals and birds, are estimated to be twenty-five hundred years old. Just to the north sprawls the 5,610-acre (2,270-hectare) Yellow River State Forest, which includes trout streams, pioneer farm buildings, and a network of hiking trails.

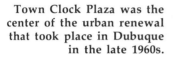

Town Clock Plaza was the center of the urban renewal that took place in Dubuque in the late 1960s.

The first white settlements in Iowa sprouted along the Mississippi. Today the docks are crowded with huge cargo barges instead of flatboats or paddle wheelers, but something of the tangy waterfront flavor still remains.

Visitors to Dubuque explore the river in style when they board the *Spirit of Dubuque* or the *Mississippi Belle*, two refurbished stern-wheelers. The Second Street Harbor complex includes the Mississippi Riverboat Museum, a Coast Guard station, and the *William M. Black*, one of the world's last side-wheeled steamboats. Dubuque's legends of pirates and smuggling are kept alive through the historical relics at the Ham House Museum. At the mouth of Catfish Creek, just south of the city, a round limestone tower marks the grave of Julien Dubuque, Iowa's first permanent white settler.

Aboard the *Spirit of Dubuque* (left), visitors to Dubuque can explore the Mississippi River (right) in style.

Each year on Good Friday, more than seven hundred people climb the winding path through the woods to the Pieta Chapel atop Calvary Hill in St. Donatus. Founded by immigrants from the tiny nation of Luxembourg, St. Donatus is the only surviving Luxembourger community in the United States.

Another place to learn about the glory days on the upper Mississippi is the City of Clinton Showboat Museum, an authentic riverboat that has been converted into a living museum on river lore. Clinton's nationally recognized Bickelhaupt Arboretum displays 782 plant species. The town of Le Claire, just south of Clinton, is famous as the birthplace of William "Buffalo Bill" Cody.

Davenport and the Illinois cities of Moline, East Moline, and Rock Island, just across the Mississippi River, form the

Snake Alley, in Burlington, has been called the "crookedest street in the world."

metropolitan area known as the Quad Cities. With its carefully preserved shops and homes, East Davenport is one of Iowa's largest historic districts. This area of Davenport has been restored to look much as it did during the 1850s. Davenport's Putnam Museum contains a wide assortment of historic exhibits, including an original treaty signed by Sauk Chief Black Hawk. Special exhibits at the Davenport Art Gallery include Mexican colonial paintings and works by midwestern artists.

Muscatine was once the world's center for the manufacture of pearl buttons. Today, visitors to the area can explore the thick woods and breathtaking rock formations at nearby Wildcat Den State Park. Weed Park—named for its founder, not its plant life—contains eighteen horseshoe-shaped burial mounds.

According to *Ripley's Believe It or Not*, Snake Alley in Burlington is the crookedest street in the world. In the course of 275 feet (84 meters), Snake Alley makes five half curves and two quarter

The Pine Creek Mill is one of the attractions of Wildcat Den State Park.

curves. Burlington's Apple Trees Museum commemorates the first apple orchard west of the Mississippi.

The Nauvoo Ferry runs daily every summer, crossing the Mississippi from Montrose to Nauvoo, Illinois. Mormons entered Iowa at Montrose in 1846, beginning their long journey across the state and west to Utah.

In 1856, the great humorist Mark Twain worked in a printing shop in Keokuk. Memorabilia of the writer's sojourn here are on display at the Miller House, a carefully restored home in this Mississippi River town.

This brief tour through the Hawkeye State can touch upon only a handful of Iowa's historic landmarks, museums, parks, and forests. Perhaps novelist Pearl Buck best summed up Iowa's role within the nation as a whole. "Without ostentation and fanfare," she wrote, "and by good organization and solid achievement, Iowa is one of our greatest and most representative states."

IOWA

FACTS AT A GLANCE

GENERAL INFORMATION

Statehood: December 28, 1846, twenty-ninth state

Origin of Name: Named for a tribe of Indians who once lived in the area and who the Sioux called the Iowa; the word has been variously interpreted to mean "one who puts to sleep" or "beautiful land"

State Capital: Des Moines

State Nickname: Hawkeye State

State Flag: Iowa's state flag has vertical stripes of blue, white, and red. In the center, an eagle with outstretched wings holds in its beak a blue ribbon with the state motto.

State Motto: "Our liberties we prize and our rights we will maintain"

State Bird: Eastern goldfinch

State Flower: Wild rose

State Colors: Red, white, and blue

State Tree: Oak

State Stone: Geode

State Song: "The Song of Iowa," words by Major S. H. M. Byers (sung to the tune of "Der Tannenbaum"):

> You ask what land I love the best,
> Iowa, 'tis Iowa.
> The fairest State of all the West,
> Iowa, O! Iowa.
> From yonder Mississippi's stream
> To where Missouri's waters gleam,
> O! Fair it is as poet's dream,
> Iowa, in Iowa.

POPULATION

Population: 2,913,808, twenty-seventh among the states (1980 census)

Population Density: 52 persons per sq. mi. (20 persons per km²)

Population Distribution: 59 percent of the state's people live in cities or towns. Although Iowa has no large cities, it has many small to medium-sized cities, such as Des Moines, Cedar Rapids, Davenport, Sioux City, and Waterloo. Main population centers are the Des Moines area, the Cedar Rapids area, and the Quad Cities area of Davenport and the three Illinois cities of Moline, East Moline, and Rock Island.

Des Moines	191,003
Cedar Rapids	110,243
Davenport	103,264
Sioux City	82,003
Waterloo	75,985
Dubuque	62,321
Council Bluffs	56,449
Iowa City	50,449
Ames	45,775
Cedar Falls	36,322

(Population figures according to 1980 census)

Population Growth: Iowa experienced rapid growth in its early years, as farmers flocked to its fertile soil. However, the state's growth has slowed and all but stopped since 1900. Iowa's population topped 2.2 million in 1900, but had reached only slightly less than 3 million in 1980.

Year	Population
1840	43,112
1860	674,913
1880	1,624,615
1900	2,231,853
1920	2,404,021
1940	2,538,268
1950	2,621,073
1960	2,757,537
1970	2,825,368
1980	2,913,808

GEOGRAPHY

Borders: Iowa is bordered by Minnesota on the north, Wisconsin and Illinois on the east, Missouri on the south, and Nebraska and South Dakota on the west.

Highest Point: In northern Osceola County, 1,670 ft. (509 m)

Lowest Point: Along the Mississippi River at Keokuk, 480 ft. (146 m)

Greatest Distances: North to south—214 mi. (344 km)
East to west—332 mi. (534 km)

Area: 56,290 sq. mi. (145,791 km²)

Rank in Area Among the States: Twenty-fifth

Rivers: Iowa's rivers have blessed this fertile state for thousands of years. No other state except neighboring Missouri owes so much to America's two major rivers. The mighty Mississippi River forms the eastern boundary of the state. The powerful Missouri forms most of the western boundary. All of Iowa's other rivers eventually flow into one of these two rivers. A western ridge forms the divide between these two basins. Rivers west of the Mississippi-Missouri Divide—such as the Floyd, Little Sioux, Boyer, West Nishnabotna, East Nishnabotna, Nodaway, Grand, Thompson, and Chariton—flow into the Missouri. The Des Moines and Iowa rivers, which drain the entire central part of the state, flow into the Mississippi. Other rivers flowing into the Mississippi include the Upper Iowa, Turkey, Maquoketa, Cedar, Wapsipinicon, and Skunk.

Lakes: Most of Iowa's natural lakes are found in the northwestern part of the state. These were formed from the advance and retreat of the last glacier. The state's largest lakes, however, are those that have been created artificially by damming rivers. These reservoirs provide flood control, electric power, and recreation. Rathbun Lake, on the Chariton River in south-central Iowa, is the state's largest lake.

Topography: Glacial activity many thousands of years ago left Iowa with three distinct land regions. The Driftless Area covers the northeastern corner of the state. Only one major glacier advanced through this area. It remains hillier than the rest of the state, with less productive soil. The Young Drift Plains cover the northern and central parts of Iowa. Four different glaciers advanced upon this area. They left the land flat, but deposited deep soil that gives this region some of the most fertile farmland on earth. Small lakes pockmark part of this region. The Dissected Till Plains cover the rest of the state. This region saw the advance of two, and in some parts, three, glaciers. Dozens of streams cut into the plains here, forming low hills, ridges, and picturesque buttes.

Climate: Iowa, like most central states, has long, hot, moist summers and harsh, cold winters. Residents know that they may see blizzards in wintertime or a tornado in the summer. Unpredictable winds may change local temperatures 50° F. (28° C) in a twenty-four-hour period. Keokuk saw the state's highest temperature, 118° F. (48° C), on July 20, 1934. The state's record low temperature, a bone-chilling -47° F. (-44° C), occurred at Washta on January 12, 1912.

A winter scene in Decorah

Des Moines sees temperatures ranging from 31° F. to 13° F. (-1° C to -11° C) in January and 87° F. to 66° F. (31° C to 19° C) in July. Sioux City experiences temperatures that range from 29° F. to 9° F. (-2° C to -13° C) in January and 88° F. to 64° F. (31° C to 18° C) in July.

Annual rainfall varies across the state, from about 26 in. (66 cm) in the north to about 36 in. (91 cm) in southern Iowa. Annual snowfall in Iowa averages about 30 in. (76 cm). Northern Iowa receives more snow than southern Iowa.

NATURE

Trees: Maple, hickory, cottonwood, elm, oak, walnut, willow, cedar, balsam, basswood, ash

Wild Plants: Aster, locoweed, shooting-star, ragwort, avens, pasqueflower, bloodroot, marsh marigold, violet, prairie lily, phlox, rose, gentian, goldenrod, prairie aster, sunflower, wild rose, milkweed, mesquite, honeysuckle, trillium, May apple, fern, pussy willow, verbena, dog fennel, quack grass, Canadian thistle

Animals: Deer, opossum, mink, muskrat, raccoon, skunk, rabbit, squirrel, coyote, fox, beaver, chipmunk, gopher, rattlesnake

Birds: Quail, pheasant, partridge, duck, Canada goose, junco, cardinal, blue jay, starling, tufted titmouse, red-winged blackbird, robin, owl, hawk, prairie chicken, grouse

Fish: Catfish, bullhead, perch, northern pike, walleye, crappie, bluegill, bass, trout, carp, buffalo, sucker

GOVERNMENT

Iowa adopted its first constitution in 1846. Another constitution replaced it in 1857. This constitution, amended about forty times, remains in effect today.

The state government, like the federal government, is divided into three branches. The legislative branch, called the general assembly, makes laws. It consists of a fifty-member senate and a one-hundred-member house of representatives. Senators serve four-year terms; representatives serve two-year terms. The general assembly begins its sessions each January, although the governor may call special sessions.

Iowa's governor heads the executive branch. Other executive branch officials include the lieutenant governor, secretary of state, auditor of state, treasurer of state, attorney general, and secretary of agriculture. All are elected to four-year terms. The governor appoints many boards and officials. Some of these appointments require the approval of the senate.

A nine-member supreme court is the highest body of the judicial branch. Each of these justices serves an eight-year term. The justices choose one of their members as chief justice. Justices of the six-member court of appeals serve six-year terms. Each of Iowa's eight judicial districts has a district court with six to twenty judges. They serve six-year terms. The district judges appoint district associate judges, who serve four-year terms. The governor appoints the justices of the supreme court, court of appeals, and district court from a list of candidates presented to him by a nominating commission. After one year, voters choose whether or not to retain these judges.

Number of Counties: 99

U.S. Representatives: 5

Electoral Votes: 8

Voting Requirements: U.S. citizen, 18 years or older, registered to vote 10 days before election

The Pleasant
Ridge Schoolhouse
in Knoxville

EDUCATION

Iowans are proud of the fact that their state has the highest literacy rate in the nation. More than 99 percent of adult Iowans can read or write. This high rate of literacy stems from the intense interest in education that Iowans have displayed since territorial days. Iowa's first school opened in 1830 in Lee County. The territorial legislature established free public schools in 1839, and the state began a system of free high schools in 1911. In 1847, Iowa's first state college, the State University of Iowa, was founded in Iowa City.

A nine-member state board of education supervises the public schools. The governor appoints board members to six-year terms. The board appoints a superintendent of public instruction. Iowa children between the ages of seven and sixteen must attend school.

The Hawkeye State has three state universities: the University of Iowa, at Iowa City (the state's largest school); Iowa State University, in Ames; and the University of Northern Iowa, in Cedar Falls. In addition, the state operates more than fifteen community colleges and vocational schools. Iowa's more than thirty private colleges include Briar Cliff College and Morningside College, in Sioux City; Central University of Iowa, in Pella; Coe College and Mount Mercy College, in Cedar Rapids; Cornell College, in Mount Vernon; Drake University and Grand View College, in Des Moines; Grinnell College, in Grinnell; Luther College, in Decorah; Simpson College, in Indianola; and William Penn College, in Oskaloosa. Dubuque has four schools: the University of Dubuque, Clarke College, Loras College, and Wartburg Theological Seminary. In Davenport are Marycrest College, St. Ambrose University, and Palmer College of Chiropractic Medicine.

A cattle farm near Iowa City

ECONOMY AND INDUSTRY

Principal Products:
Agriculture: Corn, soybeans, hogs, beef cattle, sheep, poultry, oats, rye, alfalfa, wheat, flaxseed, hay, dairy farming, barley, sorghums, potatoes, vegetables, apples, grapes, sugar beets
Manufacturing: Farm machinery, transportation equipment, metal products, processed foods, washing machines, chemicals, clothing, printed materials, rubber products, plastic products, leather products, furniture
Natural Resources: Fertile soil, coal, clay, shale, limestone, gypsum, stone, gravel, cement

Business and Trade: To many people, the first word that comes to mind when Iowa is mentioned is "corn." During the summer and early fall, visitors passing through Iowa can observe miles and miles of cornfields and understand why Iowans brag that their state is "where the tall corn grows." Iowa and neighboring Illinois engage in a friendly but spirited rivalry for the title of top corn-producing state in the nation.

Corn is not Iowa's only agricultural product, however. Although it is an average-sized state, Iowa ranks second only to the huge state of California in farm production. Most years, Iowa ranks first in the nation in livestock production. Iowa is a leading producer of beef, and leads the nation in hog production. Sheep and poultry are also raised in the state.

Grain elevators near Britt at dawn

Iowa's fertile soils produce grains that feed the United States and much of the rest of the world. In addition to corn, Iowa farmers raise wheat, oats, barley, soybeans, and hay. Processed foods, including meat products, cereals, and corn products; and farm machinery are the most important manufactured products. Food-processing plants are concentrated in Des Moines, Cedar Rapids, and Waterloo. Sioux City has the nation's largest popcorn-processing plant. Iowa also produces such varied products as ball-point pens and washing machines. The Amana Colonies, near the center of the state, are known for their fine furniture and appliances. Electrical machinery, chemicals, metal products, clothing, textiles, and paper products are other important industries.

Des Moines, Iowa's capital and largest city, is also the state's main trading center. Davenport and Dubuque are busy Mississippi River ports. Sioux City serves as a business hub for western Iowa.

Communication: Iowans have enjoyed hearty newspapers ever since the *Du Buque Visitor* was founded in 1836. Iowa's most widely circulated newspaper, the highly acclaimed *Des Moines Register*, is one of the few American papers that can boast statewide distribution. Other large dailies include the *Quad City Times* of Davenport, the *Cedar Rapids Gazette*, the *Sioux City Journal*, the *Waterloo Courier*, and Dubuque's *Telegraph-Herald*. The state has about 40 dailies and about 340 weeklies.

The University of Iowa formed the state's first radio station, WSUI, in 1919. Three years later, WOC in Davenport became the first commercial station. Today Iowa has about 180 radio stations. WOC-TV of Davenport, which first came on the air in 1949, was Iowa's first television station. In 1950, WOI-TV of Iowa State University became the nation's first commercial station owned by an educational institution. Today, Iowa has about 15 television stations.

Transportation: Rivers were Iowa's earliest "highways." Even now, river travel remains an important part of the state's transportation system. Barge traffic on Iowa's rivers accounts for about 45 million tons (41 million metric tons) of cargo

116

The State of Iowa Historical Building, in Des Moines, houses a fine historical museum, as well as the State Historical Library.

each year. Burlington, Clinton, Davenport, Dubuque, Fort Madison, Keokuk, McGregor, and Muscatine are the most important Mississippi River ports. Sioux City and Council Bluffs are the main Missouri River ports.

Railroads first opened Iowa's interior. Today, such freight lines as the Chicago & North Western, Soo, Illinois Central, and Burlington use Iowa's 4,700 mi. (7,564 km) of track.

No part of Iowa is far from a good road or highway. About 112,000 mi. (180,242 km) of roads cross the state. About 700 mi. (1,127 km) are interstate highways. I-80 is a major east-west route across the state. I-35 bisects the state from north to south. Iowa has about 355 airports. Des Moines, Cedar Rapids, Waterloo, Sioux City, and Dubuque have the largest airports. Eleven airlines serve the state.

SOCIAL AND CULTURAL LIFE

Museums: Art lovers can enjoy the nineteenth- and twentieth-century paintings at the Des Moines Art Center; the Mexican, Colonial, Oriental, and Haitian art at the Davenport Museum of Art; or the Bil Baird puppet collection at the Charles H. MacNider Museum in Mason City. The Sioux City Art Center features contemporary regional art. The Science Center of Iowa in Des Moines features a planetarium and many hands-on exhibits. The Science Station in Cedar Rapids, housed in the former Central Fire Station, is a hands-on museum that includes a giant kaleidoscope and a working hot-air balloon.

The University of Iowa has a natural history museum and an art museum. Among Iowa's many historical museums are the museum at the State of Iowa Historical Building in Des Moines; the Keokuk River Museum in Keokuk, which features items from the upper Mississippi Valley; the Apple Trees Historical Museum in Burlington, which houses the collection of the Des Moines County Historical Society; and the Wayne County Historical Museum in Corydon, which

The University of Iowa houses the state's largest library.

includes Mormon relics and a safe once robbed by Jesse James. Fort Dodge Historical Museum, in Fort Dodge, houses a replica of the 1862 fort plus a trading post, blacksmith shop, and other buildings. Other fine museums include the Ice House in Cedar Falls, the Children's Museum in Bettendorf, and the Norwegian-American Museum in Decorah.

Libraries: Iowa's first library opened in Fairfield in 1853. Today, about five hundred libraries operate throughout the state. Iowa's most famous library is the Herbert Hoover Presidential Library in West Branch, which houses documents and materials of the nation's thirty-first president. The University of Iowa houses Iowa's largest library. The library at the State of Iowa Historical Building, in Des Moines, holds state and county records, as well as rare books and manuscripts. The Iowa State Capitol has a fine law library. The Masonic Library, in Cedar Rapids, contains the nation's most complete Masonic collection.

Performing Arts: Theater, dance, and music flourish in the Hawkeye State. Several cities, including Cedar Rapids, Dubuque, Cedar Falls, and Des Moines, support symphony orchestras. The capital city is also home to the Des Moines Ballet Company and the Des Moines Community Playhouse. Every summer, opera is performed by some of the nation's finest young talent at the Des Moines Metro Opera in Indianola. Iowa State Center at Iowa State University in Ames contains an auditorium, coliseum, and theater. Clinton has a professional summer theater on a paddlewheel boat. The state's many colleges and universities sponsor a wealth of

118

The Julien Dubuque Monument marks the gravesite of Iowa's first permanent white settler.

concerts and plays. Young writers often give readings at the world-famous Writer's Workshop at the University of Iowa. The Bix Beiderbecke Jazz Festival, held every summer in Davenport, attracts jazz fans from all over the country.

Sports and Recreation: Iowa's college and high-school sports teams provide year-round excitement. The University of Iowa Hawkeyes football team is a frequent Rose Bowl contender. The Hawkeyes basketball team is a perennial Big Ten basketball power. The Iowa State Cyclones play in the mighty Big Eight conference. In the summer, Iowans can watch tomorrow's major-league baseball stars play in minor-league games in Burlington, Cedar Rapids, the Quad Cities, Des Moines, and other cities. Every August, balloonists from all over the country flock to Indianola to participate in the National Hot Air Balloon Championship. The annual Tri-State Rodeo draws crowds to Fort Madison in September. Outdoor enthusiasts can enjoy more than a hundred state-owned parks and recreation areas. The largest such park, Lacey-Keosauqua, in the southwestern part of the state, contains a wildlife preserve and recreation area.

Historic Sites and Landmarks:

General Dodge House, in Council Bluffs, was the home of Grenville Dodge, a Civil War general and the chief construction engineer for the Union Pacific Railroad.

Julien Dubuque Monument, in Dubuque, marks the gravesite of Iowa's first permanent white settler.

119

The Czech Village in Cedar Rapids

Farm House, in Ames, was the first building on the Iowa State University campus. A National Historic Landmark, it has been restored to its original splendor.

Charles Floyd Monument, in Sioux City, commemorates the only person to die during the Lewis and Clark Expedition.

Effigy Mounds National Monument, near Marquette, preserves 191 prehistoric Indian burial mounds, many of which are shaped like birds or animals.

Herbert Hoover National Historic Site, in West Branch, includes the birthplace and boyhood home of the thirty-first president.

Lewis and Clark Monument, in Council Bluffs, commemorates a council held by the explorers with Oto and Missouri Indians.

Living History Farms, near Des Moines, allows visitors to compare farms of 1840, 1900, and tomorrow.

Old Shot Tower, in Dubuque, produced lead shot during the Civil War.

Villages of Van Buren County, including Bentonsport, Keosauqua, Bonaparte, and Farmington, are historic villages that are a living monument to Iowa's steamboat era. Bentonsport National Historical District, a museum piece of mid-nineteenth-century architecture, includes the state's oldest post office.

The Boone & Scenic Valley Railroad

Other Interesting Places to Visit:

Amana Colonies are seven villages operated by a religious society that produces high-quality food products, furniture, and appliances.

Boone & Scenic Valley Railroad, in Boone, offers a train ride through the scenic Des Moines Valley over the route of the former Fort Dodge, Des Moines, & Southern Railroad.

Czech Village, in Cedar Rapids, has historic structures, bakeries, and restaurants preserving Czech heritage.

Danish Windmill, in Elk Horn, is an original windmill that was made in Denmark in 1848, dismantled, shipped to Iowa, and rebuilt.

DeSoto National Wildlife Refuge, in Missouri Valley, is a major stopover for geese and ducks migrating along the Missouri River Valley. The refuge's visitors' center features wildlife exhibits and artifacts from a sunken Missouri River steamboat.

Fenelon Place Elevator, in Dubuque, features one of the world's shortest, steepest incline railways.

Grotto of the Redemption, in West Bend, depicts the Biblical story of the fall and redemption of man through ornamental stones from many countries.

The Fenelon Place Elevator, in Dubuque, features one of the world's shortest and steepest incline railways.

Heritage Trail, near Dubuque, provides 25 mi. (40 km) of hiking, biking, and cross-country skiing along an old railroad line.

Iowa Arboretum, near Ames, contains hundreds of varieties of plants amidst scenic trails, ravines, and streams.

Klokkenspel, at Franklin Place in Pella, is a Dutch-style musical clock tower with figures representing the town's early history.

Old Capitol, in Iowa City, the state's first capitol, has been restored to its 1840s appearance.

State Capitol, in Des Moines, completed in 1871, contains a towering central dome, paintings, mosaics, and a collection of war flags.

University of Northern Iowa, in Cedar Falls, is noted for its Italian Renaissance-style campanile (bell tower).

Victorian Row, in Council Bluffs, contains specialty shops in late nineteenth-century homes.

IMPORTANT DATES

c. 500 B.C.—Mound-building civilization thrives

1673—French explorers Father Jacques Marquette and Louis Jolliet become the first Europeans to visit Iowa

1679—Daniel Greysolon, Sieur Duluth, claims the Upper Mississippi region for France

1680—Michel Accault and Father Louis Hennepin travel along the Iowa shore of the Mississippi

1682—René-Robert Cavelier, Sieur de La Salle, claims the entire Mississippi River Valley, including the land of present-day Iowa, for France; he names it Louisiana after French King Louis XIV

1733—Sauk and Mesquakie Indians flee to Iowa after being forced out of Wisconsin by the French

1735—French soldiers under Des Noyelles battle Sac and Mesquakie Indians near present-day Des Moines

1762—France cedes the Louisiana territory west of the Mississippi River to Spain

1781—Lead is discovered in present-day Iowa

1788—Fur trader Julien Dubuque obtains permission from the Mesquakie to work the lead mines

1800—Spain cedes Louisiana to France

1803—The U.S. purchases the Louisiana region, including Iowa, from France for $15 million

1804—Meriwether Lewis and William Clark pass through Iowa on their expedition to the Pacific Ocean

1805—Zebulon Pike passes the Iowa shore while traveling up the Mississippi River

1808—Fort Madison, the first U.S. military outpost in the Iowa region, is built

1812—Congress makes the Iowa region part of Missouri Territory

1820—Congress's passage of the Missouri Compromise makes Iowa a free (nonslave) territory

1830—Dr. Isaac Galland establishes the first school in Iowa

1832—Sauk and Mesquakie Indians led by Chief Black Hawk battle the U.S. Army in the Black Hawk War; after their defeat, the Indians cede to the U.S. government a strip of land west of the Mississippi River that becomes known as the Black Hawk Purchase

1833—Permanent white settlement begins in the Iowa region

1834—Iowa becomes part of Michigan Territory; Fort Des Moines is established at the confluence of the Des Moines and Mississippi rivers

1836—Wisconsin Territory, which includes the land of present-day Iowa, is established; the *Du Buque Visitor*, Iowa's first newspaper, begins publication

1838—Iowa Territory is established

1839—The territorial legislature sets up a system of common schools; Iowa City becomes the territorial capital

1841—The territorial legislature convenes in Iowa City for the first time

1844—The first state constitutional convention meets in Iowa City

1846—Iowa enters the Union as the twenty-ninth state

1847—The University of Iowa, at Iowa City, is chartered

1850—Hungarians found a colony at New Buda

1853—Iowa's first public library opens at Fairfield

1855—The Amana colony is established in Iowa; the University of Iowa opens

1857—Iowa voters adopt the present state constitution; the state capital is moved to Des Moines

1858—Iowa State Agricultural College and Model Farm (now Iowa State University) in Ames is chartered

1862—Congress passes the Homestead Act

1867—The first railroad across the state is completed

1868—An amendment to the state constitution gives black males the right to vote

1869—Iowan Anabella Bobb Mansfield becomes the first woman admitted to the practice of law in the U.S.

1884—Present state capitol opens

1890 — Iowa becomes the nation's leading producer of corn

1891 — The manufacture of pearl buttons begins at Muscatine

1913 — Engineers complete the Keokuk Dam

1917 — The state begins an extensive road-building program

1919 — WSUI, probably the first radio station west of the Mississippi River, begins broadcasting in Iowa City

1928 — Iowan Herbert Hoover is elected president of the U.S.

1931 — In what becomes known as the "Cow War," state militia are called out to enforce a program to test Iowa dairy cattle for tuberculosis; Iowan Susan Glaspell wins the Pulitizer Prize in drama for *Alison's House*

1940 — Iowan Henry Wallace is elected vice-president under President Franklin D. Roosevelt

1946 — Iowan John Mott wins the Nobel Peace Prize for his YMCA work and for aiding displaced persons

1953 — The state legislature creates a nine-member state board of education to administer the public schools

1956 — Iowan Mackinlay Kantor wins the Pulitzer Prize in fiction for *Andersonville*

1962 — Iowa reorganizes its court system

1970 — Iowan Norman Borlaug wins the Nobel Peace Prize for helping increase food production in developing countries

1989 — A plane crash in Sioux City kills 111 passengers, although skilled maneuvering by the crew saves many passengers' lives

FRAN ALLISON

CAP ANSON

GEORGE BARNARD

BIX BEIDERBECKE

IMPORTANT PEOPLE

Fran Allison (1907-1989), born in La Porte City; entertainer; hosted the pioneer children's television series "Kukla, Fran, and Ollie"

William Boyd Allison (1829-1908), politician; U.S. representative from Iowa (1862-70); U.S. senator (1872-1908); headed the powerful Senate Appropriations Committee for nearly thirty years

Adrian Constantine (Cap) Anson (1852-1922), born in Marshalltown; professional baseball player; known as the greatest baseball player of the nineteenth century; became the first major-league player to make 3,000 hits; led the Chicago White Stockings to five pennants

Jack Bailey (1907-1980), born in Hampton; television host; served as master of ceremonies for such programs as "Queen for a Day," "Truth or Consequences," and "Place the Face"

Richard Achilles Ballinger (1858-1922), born in Boonesboro; lawyer, politician; secretary of the interior under President William Howard Taft (1909-11); resigned after foes charged that he opposed conservation policies

Dave Bancroft (1891-1972), born in Sioux City; professional baseball player; shortstop who helped lead the Phillies and Giants to four pennants; elected to Baseball Hall of Fame (1971)

George Grey Barnard (1863-1938), sculptor; grew up in Muscatine; most famous work was *Struggle of Two Natures of Man*

Carl Lotus Becker (1873-1945), born in Black Hawk County; historian, professor; specialized in the American Revolutionary period; wrote *The Eve of the Revolution, The Declaration of Independence*, and *Progress and Power*

Leon Bismarck (Bix) Beiderbecke (1903-1931), born in Davenport; cornet player, pianist, composer; thrilled audiences with his jazz solos; performed with many great jazz bands but won acclaim from peers for his small jazz combos; composed "Singin' the Blues" and "In a Mist"

Black Hawk (1767-1838), Sauk Indian chief; fought on the side of the British during War of 1812; refused to move west of the Mississippi River, contending that his people had been duped into signing the 1804 treaty that ceded their lands east of the Mississippi to the U.S. government; to defend the Indian lands, fought the Black Hawk War (1832), which ended in defeat for the Indians; spent final years on a Des Moines River Indian reservation

Amelia Jenks Bloomer (1818-1894), social reformer; settled in Council Bluffs; advocated prohibition and women's rights; popularized loose-fitting pants for women that came to be known as "bloomers"; headed the Iowa Woman Suffrage Association

Norman Ernest Borlaug (1914-   ), born in Cresco; agronomist; developed new varieties of wheat that could adapt to warmer climates; in the 1950s and 1960s, the types of wheat he developed were introduced to Mexico, India, and Pakistan; helped change several countries from grain importers to grain exporters; won 1970 Nobel Peace Prize for his food-production efforts

Ansel Briggs (1806-1881), politician; first governor of Iowa (1846-50); fought for a free school system and teachers' college; settled a boundary dispute with Missouri

Johnny Carson (1925-   ), born in Corning; entertainer; host of the long-running television show the "Tonight Show"

Carrie Chapman Catt (1859-1947), social reformer; served as principal and superintendent of Mason City, Iowa, schools; helped form the Iowa Woman Suffrage Association; president of National American Woman Suffrage Association (1900-04, 1915-47); led the campaign that resulted in ratification of Nineteenth Amendment to the Constitution (1920), which gave women the right to vote

William Frederick "Buffalo Bill" Cody (1846-1917), born in Scott County; frontiersman, scout, showman; scouted and hunted buffalo for the federal government; earned the nickname "Buffalo Bill" for his outstanding marksmanship; formed Buffalo Bill's Wild West Show, which toured the U.S. and Europe

Lee De Forest (1873-1961), born in Council Bluffs; inventor; created transmitting and receiving devices that earned him the nickname "Father of Radio"; equipped U.S. Navy ships with wireless telephones; pioneered the transatlantic telephone; inaugurated news broadcasts by radio

Julien Dubuque (1762-1810), pioneer; Iowa's first white settler; convinced the Mesquakie Indians to allow him to work lead mines in the Iowa region; started a lead mine in 1788 that he named the "Mines of Spain"

Urban (Red) Faber (1888-1976), born in Cascade; professional baseball player; won 254 major-league games with the Chicago White Sox, including three in the 1917 World Series; led American League in earned-run average twice; entered Baseball Hall of Fame in 1964

Robert William Andrew Feller (1918-   ), born in Van Meter; professional baseball player; threw three no-hitters and 12 one-hitters; won 266 major-league games as fireball pitcher with Cleveland Indians; led American League in strikeouts seven times; elected to Baseball Hall of Fame in 1962

AMELIA BLOOMER

CARRIE CHAPMAN CATT

WILLIAM CODY

RED FABER

WILLIAM FRAWLEY

SUSAN GLASPELL

HERBERT HOOVER

HARRY HOPKINS

William Frawley (1887-1966), born in Burlington; actor; portrayed grouchy neighbor Fred Mertz in the classic television series "I Love Lucy"

George Gallup (1901-1984), born in Jefferson; public-opinion expert; founded the American Institute of Public Opinion, which created the famous Gallup Poll

Hamlin Garland (1860-1940), author; spent much of his childhood on the Iowa frontier; drew on his early experiences to write books that expressed the cruel hardships of pioneer life; best known works include *Main-Travelled Roads, A Son of the Middle Border* (his autobiography), and *A Daughter of the Middle Border,* which won the 1922 Pulitzer Prize in biography

Susan Glaspell (1882-1948), born in Davenport; novelist, playwright; with her husband, founded the prestigious Provincetown Playhouse; won the 1930 Pulitzer Prize in drama for *Alison's House*; other plays include *Suppressed Desires* and *Bernice*; also wrote a number of novels, including *Lifted Masks* and *The Morning Is Near Us*

Fred Grandy (1948-), born in Sioux City; actor, politician; played the character of Gopher in the television series "The Love Boat"; U.S. representative from Iowa (1987-)

James Wilson Grimes (1816-1872), politician; helped form the Republican party in Iowa; governor of Iowa (1854-57); U.S. senator from Iowa (1859-69)

Josiah Bushnell Grinnell (1821-1891), clergyman, pioneer, politician, abolitionist; moved from New England to Iowa (1854); founded the town of Grinnell; helped found the college that became Grinnell College; U.S. representative from Iowa (1863-67)

Herbert Clark Hoover (1874-1964), born in West Branch; thirty-first president of the United States; made a fortune as a geologist and engineer; during World War I, served as head of the American Relief Commission in London (1914-15) and Commission for Relief in Belgium (1915-19); U.S. secretary of commerce under President Calvin Coolidge (1921-29); U.S. president (1929-33)

Harry Lloyd Hopkins (1890-1946), born in Sioux City; statesman; directed Red Cross and other social welfare agencies; distributed $8.5 billion to the unemployed as director of the Federal Emergency Relief Administration and the Works Progress Administration; was President Franklin D. Roosevelt's closest advisor; U.S. secretary of commerce (1938-40)

Mackinlay Kantor (1904-1977), born in Webster City; author; wrote many books with Civil War themes; won the 1956 Pulitzer Prize in fiction for *Andersonville*; other books include *Long Remember* and *Spirit Lake*, based on Iowa's 1857 Spirit Lake Massacre

Keokuk (1780?-1848), Sauk Indian leader; established a tribal claim to present-day Iowa for Sauk Indians; a rival of Black Hawk, he helped the Americans during the Black Hawk War (1832); arranged peace between the Sauk and the Sioux (1837); the town of Keokuk is named in his honor

Samuel J. Kirkwood (1813-1894), politician; governor of Iowa (1860-64, 1876-77); governed Iowa during Civil War, keeping the state in the Union; used his own funds to buy arms for the war; U.S. secretary of the interior under President James A. Garfield (1881-87)

SAMUEL KIRKWOOD

Ann Landers (1918-   ), born Esther "Eppie" Friedman in Sioux City; newspaper columnist; writes a daily advice column that is syndicated in newspapers throughout the nation

William Larrabee (1832-1912), businessman, politician; governor of Iowa (1886-90); U.S. senator from Iowa (1867-   ); one of Iowa's strongest governors, he fought the liquor trade and helped regulate railroads

ANN LANDERS

Cloris Leachman (1926-   ), born in Des Moines; actress; character actress who has appeared in many films; won an Academy Award for best supporting actress for her role in *The Last Picture Show* (1971); winner of five Emmy awards; also known for her portrayal of Phyllis Lindstrom in the television programs "The Mary Tyler Moore Show" and "Phyllis"

William Daniel Leahy (1875-1959), born in Hampton; naval officer; served in the Spanish-American War, Boxer Rebellion, Nicaraguan occupation, and World War I; chief of the Navy Bureau of Ordnance (1927-31); chief of naval operations (1937-39); ambassador to France (1940-42); Admiral of the Fleet during World War II; presidential chief of staff (1942-49)

WILLIAM LEAHY

John Llewellyn Lewis (1880-1969), born near Lucas; labor leader; headed the United Mine Workers' Union for forty years (1920-60); called for the first industry-wide coal strike; formed the Congress of Industrial Organizations; secured welfare funds for miners that were financed entirely by management but controlled by the union

Robert Lucas (1781-1853), politician; first territorial governor of Iowa; encouraged public education, railroad growth, and temperance

Anabella Bobb Mansfield (1846-1911), born near Burlington; lawyer, teacher; in 1869, became the first woman admitted to the practice of law in the U.S.; taught English and history at Iowa Wesleyan University; helped form the Iowa Woman Suffrage Association

JOHN L. LEWIS

GLENN MILLER

HARRY REASONER

CHARLES RINGLING

LILLIAN RUSSELL

Jerry Mathers (1948-   ), born in Sioux City; actor; played Theodore "Beaver" Cleaver in the television series "Leave It to Beaver"

Elsa Maxwell (1883-1963), born in Keokuk; socialite, writer; mingled with celebrities and hosted lavish Hollywood parties during the 1930s, 1940s, and 1950s; wrote *I Married the World* and *Celebrity Circus*

Glenn Miller (1904-1944), born in Clarinda; trombonist, composer, bandleader; led one of the most famous "Big Bands" of the 1930s and 1940s; composed such famous songs as "In the Mood," "Tuxedo Junction," "Little Brown Jug," "Moonlight Serenade," and "Sunrise Serenade"

John Raleigh Mott (1865-1955), religious leader; with Emily Balch, won the 1946 Nobel Peace Prize for his work with the YMCA and his efforts to aid prisoners of war; became first chairman of the International Missionary Council; served as honorary chairman of the World Council of Churches

Harriet Hilliard Nelson (1914-   ), born Peggy Lou Snyder in Des Moines; actress; with her real-life husband Ozzie Nelson, starred in the radio (and later television) program "The Adventures of Ozzie and Harriet"

Herbert Quick (1861-1925), born in Grundy County; author; wrote *Vandemark's Folly* and other novels describing early Iowa's log-cabin communities

Robert Ray (1928-   ), born in Des Moines; politician; longest-serving governor in Iowa history (1969-83); chairman of the National Governors Conference

Harry Reasoner (1923-   ), television journalist; longtime network news anchor; host of the acclaimed television series "60 Minutes"; won four Emmy awards, including the 1974 award for Television News Broadcaster of the Year

Donna Reed (1921-1986), born in Denison; actress; starred in the classic film *It's a Wonderful Life*; starred in the television series "The Donna Reed Show"

Alfred (1861-1919), **Charles** (1863-1926) and **John** (1866-1936) **Ringling**, all born in MacGregor; circus owners; organized, with their brothers Albert and Otto, the Ringling Brothers Circus; combined with the Barnum and Bailey Circus to provide the biggest show in the world; employed some five thousand people and hundreds of animals for their "big top" shows

Lillian Russell (1861-1922), born Helen Louise Leonard in Clinton; singer; known for her ravishing beauty; began her career as an opera singer; later became a popular singer and comedienne; starred in comic operas, musical shows, and vaudeville; raised thousands of dollars for the Red Cross and Liberty Loan campaigns during World War I

Dred Scott (1795?-1858), Missouri-born slave who was taken to Iowa; the U.S. Supreme Court ruled in an 1857 decision that Scott must be returned to his owner, an event that helped trigger the Civil War

DRED SCOTT

Carl Emil Seashore (1866-1949), psychologist; at the University of Iowa, did pioneering research on musical ability and scientific testing of hearing; wrote several influential books, including *Psychology of Music*

Ruth Suckow (1892-1960), author; lived in Iowa and drew on her experiences there to write a number of novels, including *Country People*, a multigenerational saga of an Iowa family

JAMES VAN ALLEN

William Ashley (Billy) Sunday (1862-1935), born in Ames; evangelist; left his career as a baseball outfielder to preach throughout the country; attracted thousands at his meetings, becoming the best-known minister of his time

James Alfred Van Allen (1914-   ), born in Mount Pleasant; physicist; head of the department of physics and astronomy at the University of Iowa (1951-85); developed the proximity fuse, which detonates if it passes near a target; invented the cosmic ray detection device, which discovered the two radiation belts around the earth that are now called the Van Allen belts; organized the International Geophysical Year of 1957-58

Abigail Van Buren (1918-   ), born Pauline Friedman in Sioux City; newspaper columnist; twin sister of Ann Landers; her "Dear Abby" advice column appears daily in newspapers throughout the country

HENRY A. WALLACE

Arthur Charles "Dazzy" Vance (1891-1961), born in Orient; professional baseball player; pitcher who led the National League in victories, earned-run average, and strikeouts in 1924; led league in strikeouts seven times with Brooklyn Dodgers; elected to Baseball Hall of Fame (1955)

Henry Agard Wallace (1888-1965), born in Adair County; politician; U.S. secretary of agriculture (1933-40); vice-president of the U.S. under President Franklin D. Roosevelt (1941-45); U.S. secretary of commerce (1945-46); Progressive party candidate for president in 1948; editor of the *New Republic* (1946-47)

Henry Cantwell Wallace (1866-1924), publisher, author, government official; father of Henry Agard Wallace; editor of *Wallace's Farmer*, a leading agricultural journal; U.S. secretary of agriculture under Presidents Warren G. Harding and Calvin Coolidge (1921-24)

JOHN WAYNE

John Wayne (1907-1979), born Marion Michael Morrison in Winterset; actor; made nearly 200 films; became an American legend by portraying strong, heroic men in such films as *Stagecoach, Red River, Sands of Iwo Jima,* and *True Grit*, for which he won an Academy Award for best actor (1969)

GRANT WOOD

Andy Williams (1930-   ), born in Wall Lake; singer; sang "Canadian Sunset," "Hawaiian Wedding Song," and "Moon River"; hosted several television variety shows in the 1960s and 1970s

Meredith Willson (1902-1984), born in Mason City; composer, lyricist; wrote the famed Broadway musical *The Music Man*, using his hometown as the basis for fictional River City, Iowa

Garfield Arthur Wood (1880-1971), born in Mapleton; sportsman, industrialist, boat builder; set world records in speedboat and hydroplane racing; won the Harmsworth Trophy for hydroplane racing eight times; devised the PT boat used in World War II

Grant Wood (1892-1942), born in Anamosa; artist; using a sharply realistic style, portrayed people and activities of the Midwest; best known work is *American Gothic*, a painting of a midwestern farmer and his daughter

GOVERNORS

Ansel Briggs	1846-1850	Nathan E. Kendall	1921-1925
Stephen Hempstead	1850-1854	John Hammill	1925-1931
James Wilson Grimes	1854-1858	Daniel W. Turner	1931-1933
Ralph P. Lowe	1858-1860	Clyde L. Herring	1933-1937
Samuel J. Kirkwood	1860-1864	Nelson G. Kraschel	1937-1939
William M. Stone	1864-1868	George A. Wilson	1939-1943
Samuel Merrill	1868-1872	Bourke B. Hickenlooper	1943-1945
Cyrus C. Carpenter	1872-1876	Robert D. Blue	1945-1949
Samuel J. Kirkwood	1876-1877	William S. Beardsley	1949-1954
Joshua G. Newbold	1877-1878	Leo Elthon	1954-1955
John H. Gear	1878-1882	Leo A. Hoegh	1955-1957
Buren R. Sherman	1882-1886	Herschel C. Loveless	1957-1961
William Larrabee	1886-1890	Norman A. Erbe	1961-1963
Horace Boies	1890-1894	Harold E. Hughs	1963-1969
Frank Darr Jackson	1894-1896	Robert Ray	1969-1983
Francis M. Drake	1896-1898	Terry Branstad	1983-
Leslie M. Shaw	1898-1902		
Albert B. Cummins	1902-1908		
Warren Garst	1908-1909		
Beryl F. Carroll	1909-1913		
George W. Clarke	1913-1917		
William L. Harding	1917-1921		

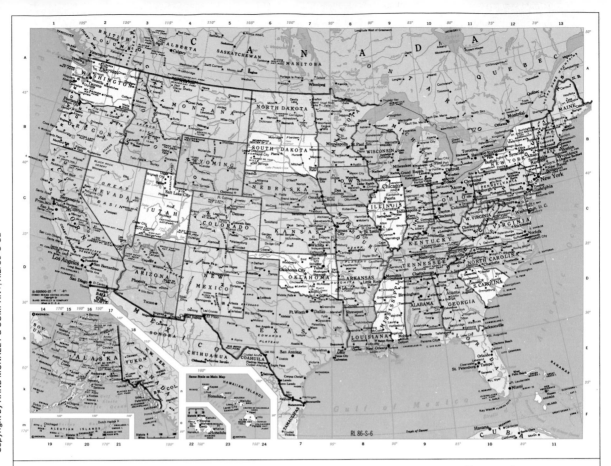

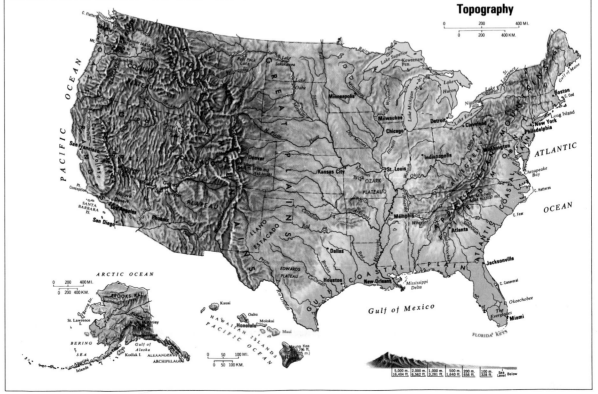

Topography

From *Cosmopolitan World Atlas* © 1990 by Rand McNally, R.L. 90-S-252

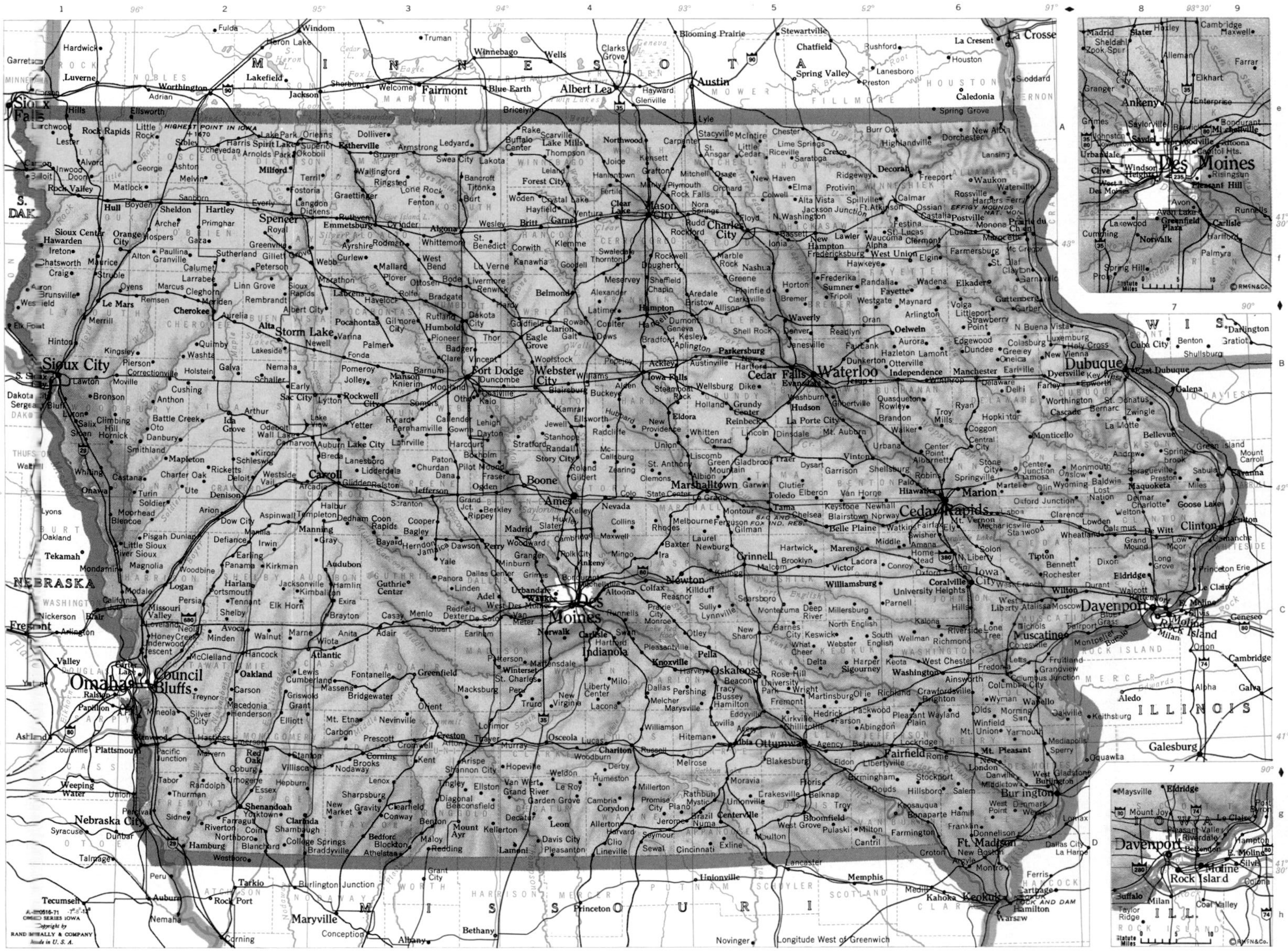
MINNESOTA
WISCONSIN
ILLINOIS
MISSOURI
NEBRASKA
S. DAK.
Des Moines
Sioux City
Council Bluffs
Omaha
Cedar Rapids
Waterloo
Davenport
Dubuque
Mason City
Fort Dodge
Ames
Iowa City
Burlington
Ottumwa
Rock Island
Longitude West of Greenwich
HIGHEST POINT IN IOWA
Statute Miles

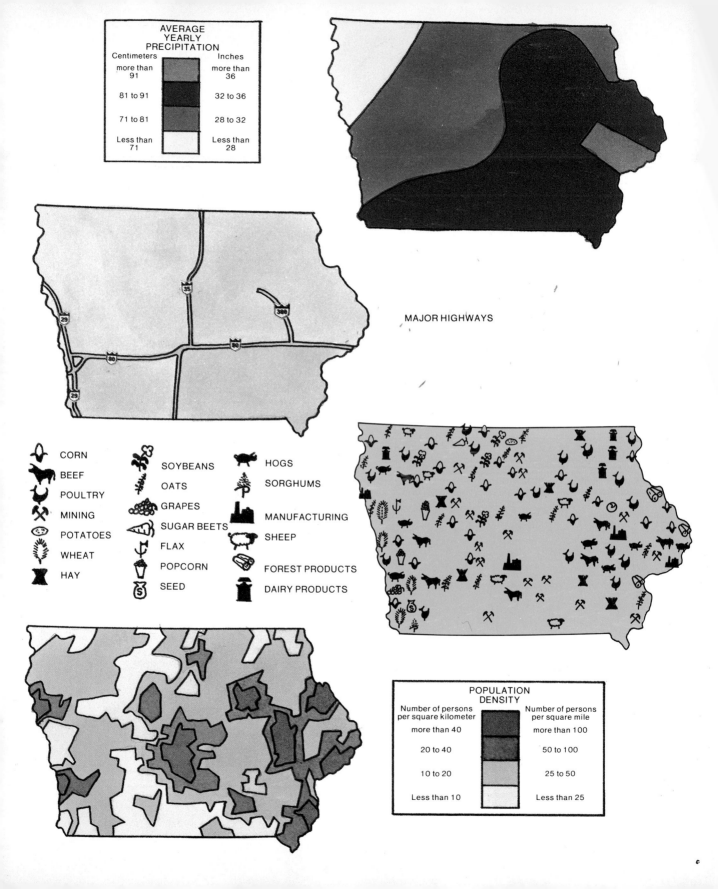

AVERAGE
YEARLY
PRECIPITATION

Centimeters | Inches

more than 91 | more than 36

81 to 91 | 32 to 36

71 to 81 | 28 to 32

Less than 71 | Less than 28

MAJOR HIGHWAYS

CORN
BEEF
POULTRY
MINING
POTATOES
WHEAT
HAY

SOYBEANS
OATS
GRAPES
SUGAR BEETS
FLAX
POPCORN
SEED

HOGS
SORGHUMS
MANUFACTURING
SHEEP
FOREST PRODUCTS
DAIRY PRODUCTS

POPULATION
DENSITY

Number of persons per square kilometer | Number of persons per square mile

more than 40 | more than 100

20 to 40 | 50 to 100

10 to 20 | 25 to 50

Less than 10 | Less than 25

TOPOGRAPHY

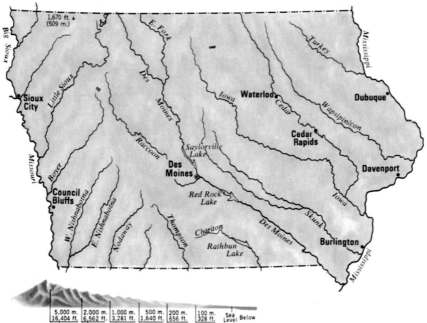

5,000 m. | 2,000 m. | 1,000 m. | 500 m. | 200 m. | 100 m. | Sea | Below
16,404 ft. | 6,562 ft. | 3,281 ft. | 1,640 ft. | 656 ft. | 328 ft. | Level |

Courtesy of Hammond, Incorporated
Maplewood, New Jersey

COUNTIES

An overhead view of Lansing

INDEX

Page numbers that appear in boldface type indicate illustrations

Canoeing on the backwaters of the Mississippi

Picture Identifications

Front cover: Fields in central Iowa
Pages 2-3: Sunrise at Cedar Hills Sand Prairie in Black Hawk County
Page 6: A Cornfield in Decorah
Pages 8-9: St. Donatus
Pages 18-19: Montage of Iowa residents
Page 24: Effigy Mounds National Monument
Page 40: A man demonstrating midwestern farming methods of old at the Living History Farms in Des Moines
Page 54: President Herbert Hoover (right) arriving in Davenport and being greeted by Iowa Governor Dan Turner during Hoover's campaign for re-election in 1932
Pages 66-77: The Iowa State Capitol in Des Moines
Pages 76-77: *Fall Plowing*, By Grant Wood
Pages 86-87: The Henry Wallace Building reflecting the Iowa State Capitol in Des Moine
Page 108: Montage of state symbols, including the state flag, tree (oak), flower (wild rose), bird (eastern goldfinch), and stone (geode)
Back cover: Des Moines

About the Author

Deborah Kent grew up in Little Falls, New Jersey, and received her B.A. from Oberlin College. She earned a master's degree in social work from Smith College School for Social Work, and worked for four years at the University Settlement House on New York's Lower East Side. She spent five years in San Miguel de Allende, Mexico, where she earned a master's in fine arts at the Instituto Allende and began her career as a writer.

Ms. Kent is the author of a dozen novels for young adults, as well as several titles in the *America the Beautiful* series. She lives in Chicago with her husband and their daughter Janna.

Picture Acknowledgments

144